DARWIN

an evolutionary entertainment

NCQ TITLES

*Though each can be read independently,
these NCQ publications, taken together,
comprise a single hyper-text collection*

DARWIN

AN EVOLUTIONARY
ENTERTAINMENT

Bernard Sharratt

New Crisis Quarterly
2015

NEW CRISIS QUARTERLY

ncq@newcrisisquarterly.myzen.co.uk

First published 2015

ISBN : 978-1-910956-19-9

For
one-time
colleagues & students
at
Darwin College
University of Kent
Canterbury UK

This play was originally written in 1982, as part of the celebrations for the 150th anniversary of Charles Darwin's death. It was drafted in collaboration with students and staff from Darwin College, the University of Kent, and was produced at the Gulbenkian Theatre, Canterbury.

The revised version dates mainly from 2009, and was submitted to the National Theatre in London, partly with an eye on the 100th anniversary of the crucial 1909 committee which eventually led to that theatre and partly with the 150th anniversary of *The Origin of Species*.in mind. It was envisaged as one of a trilogy of plays, one for each NT auditorium: *Darwin* to be played in the traditional proscenium-arch Lyttelton, alongside *Last Priest of Horus* in the Olivier, with its classical open stage and marvellous drum revolve, and *Strange Meetings* in the flexible Cottesloe studio space. Needless to say, the National Theatre, after some consideration, wisely declined this unique staging opportunity. Since, however, this play itself playfully deploys a range of theatrical and dramatic modes, its text version invites the reader to stage it, in imagination, in a variety of possible theatrical forms.

A play-text is a particularly suitable form for the 'New Crisis Quarterly' imprint, since that name revives the title of an extremely short-lived periodical, whose first, only, and final issue originally appeared in 1984, under the guise of *The Literary Labyrinth*. Its editorial programme was to publish reviews of imagined books I didn't feel that I then had the time actually to write, so its readers were cheerfully invited, if so inclined, to write those works themselves. In the same spirit, reading a play-text means that most of the work of imagining an actual performance can be left to you, which is part of the fun of writing one.

B.S.
May Day
2015

[PROLOGUE]

Completely bare stage. Dark.
Brief snatch of Beethoven, Piano Concerto No 5, Emperor.
Music ends.
Lights up to low level.
A large multi-coloured ball bounces 3 or 4 times
across from stage left to stage right,
and disappears into the wings.

CHILD dances cheerfully across from stage left
to stage right, skipping, and chasing after the ball.

The Child is a boy of about 8, dressed in early 19th century
knickerbockers, a cross between Gainsborough's Boy in Blue
and Millais' Bubbles.
Wears the face-mask of Comedy, which might also be that of an ape.

Child giggles as he exits SR, following the ball out of sight.

Lights up full.

Clearly audible rumble of moving Platform as it slowly wheels forward
from rear of stage. On the large, low, wooden Platform are:

Charles DARWIN, aged 18
and BLACKIE, 60 year-old, grey-haired black man.

Both are seated on an old wooden bench. Both wear leather aprons,
freshly bloodstained. Darwin has the carcase of large bird (a white
barnacle goose) on his knees and is extracting parts of its innards with
a knife. A bloody business.

In front of the bench is a large tin basin containing the innards
extracted so far.

Upstage from the bench, on the platform, is a rain-barrel.
Rest of the stage is bare.

As the Platform reaches the central playing position, three rigid banners fly in, to form a quasi-proscenium opening around the Platform, echoing late medieval itinerant stages, William Poel's fit-up theatre, and Chinese banners in a Brechtian production.

On horizontal banner, above centre:
MR DARWIN LEARNS A LESSON
On vertical banner, stage left: EDINBURGH
On vertical banner, stage right: 28TH MARCH 1828

[SCENE ONE]

Darwin speaks first, casually,
as if continuing a conversation after an easy silence.

> DARWIN
> I caught a sea mouse down on the shore this morning. I touched its mouth and it tried to coil itself into a ball. Like a frightened hedgehog. But in a curiously lazy way. A kind of inert effort. Linnaeus classifies it as Aphrodita Aculeata. Prickly Venus.

Blackie is watching Darwin at work on the bird.
He interrupts, relaxed, casual:

> BLACKIE
> Why 'Venus'?

> DARWIN
> I honestly don't know. It's rather difficult to imagine the love-life of a diminutive sea mouse, isn't it! Linnaeus says it has four feelers—but Turton states quite definitely that it only has two. I observed four myself, but perhaps there are two different species...

> BLACKIE
> *(Interrupts sharply and reaches over to examine bird.)*

No, not that way, Mr. Darwin. Make sure you take it all out. If you don't clean it thoroughly, the bird will eventually rot. Use the very edge of the knife.

DARWIN
Show me exactly.

Darwin hands the carcase over to Blackie, who scrapes the inside thoroughly, and hands it back.

BLACKIE
Mr Darwin, why you want to learn this technique?

DARWIN
Well, I do think Waterton's method gives the best results, as far as I can judge.

BLACKIE
I meant, why learn taxidermy at all? A doctor surely doesn't need to know how to stuff dead animals. Will you pickle your favourite patients when you fail to cure them, keep them in glass cases in your surgery?

DARWIN *(laughs)*
No, my dear Blackie—I'll never be a doctor anyway. I'm only a medical student because my father thought I might follow in his profession.

BLACKIE
Then what will you be? A taxidermist?

DARWIN
(Continues working on the bird; thetone is casual, friendly, ruminating:) No, no. But I can't decide— Certainly not a doctor. I've only seen two operations performed and they truly sickened me. The second was on a child—I realise now why my father feels ill every time he has to operate.

Perhaps a clergyman. Father finally agreed to my
going to Cambridge next year only if I seriously
considered entering the ministry. But one doesn't
know—There. I think that's well cleaned out.

BLACKIE
Yes. Excellent. You are a good pupil.

DARWIN
And you are a good teacher, Blackie.
It's a strange combination of choice and chance,
I suppose, what one becomes. You never thought
you would one day be teaching a medical student
how to stuff dead animals.

BLACKIE
It was *only* chance in my case.
A slave doesn't think he can choose his own future.
But you have that freedom.

DARWIN
Provided my father will finance it, of course!
Do you ever want to go back home, Blackie?
Reading Waterton's book on South America,
I thought how marvellous it might be to live there.
Do you ever regret that he brought you to Europe
with him?

BLACKIE
No regrets. Mr Waterton was very good to me.
But I have no home—or father - to go back to.
I don't know where I really came from.
I simply belonged to Mr Waterton.

DARWIN
Yes, I partly understand. *(pause)* My mother died
when I was eight. All I remember of her is that she
once told me, that if I looked very closely into the
inside of a blossom, I would find the name of the

flower there. I thought that was quite wonderful.
But I didn't understand what she meant.
And neither did my teachers.

> BLACKIE
>
> Perhaps—

*He is interrupted by the agitated entrance of W.A. Browne,
a somewhat dandified but energetic young gentleman,
aged 20. Browne steps onto the Platform.
Blackie stands in deference, Darwin remains seated.*

> BROWNE
>
> My dear Darwin. So that's where you are.
> Good Lord, what on earth are you doing?
> Your landlady told me you were in the yard
> but she didn't tell me you were preparing dinner!

> DARWIN *(laughs)*
>
> No, my dear Browne. I am ardently pursuing
> my studies. Let me introduce the most learned
> servant of the noble Professor Duncan, who has
> been kindly instructing me in the arcane rites of
> Watertonian taxidermy.

> BROWNE
>
> In what? You're quite impossible, Darwin.
> *(turns to Blackie, but does not offer to shake hands:)*
> Duncan's man, eh. Well you can tell your noble
> master from me that his lectures are positively
> purgatorial. *(to Darwin:)* A whole hour this morning,
> before breakfast—on the pointless, interminable
> properties of rhubarb! *(to Blackie:)* No, perhaps
> you'd better not tell him. *(to Darwin:)* Look, Darwin,
> I have something most decidedly urgent to ask you.
> Have you finished this—this sanguinary exercise,
> whatever it is?

DARWIN *(laughs)*
Yes, yes, my most impatient Browne.
We can finish for the day.
(to Blackie) Will you be free at five tomorrow?

BLACKIE *(more formal now)*
Yes, Master Darwin. At five.
Shall I take your apron?

DARWIN
Please.

*Both take off their aprons. Darwin is now dressed as a gentleman,
Blackie as a servant. Blackie collects the carcase, the tin with entrails,
etc. Browne is impatient.*

BLACKIE *(on point of going)*
Perhaps, Master Darwin— *(hesitates)* Perhaps, sir,
your mother was attempting to teach you Linnaeus's
method of classification: the name of the plant
in the arrangement of the pistil and stamen.
Tomorrow at five.

Blackie steps off the platform, and exits, rear.

BROWNE *(bewildered)*
What an extraordinary remark!

DARWIN
Though I do believe he may be right.

Darwin goes to the rainbarrel and begins to wash blood from his hands.

BROWNE
Look, Darwin, this really is most important.
It's an outrage and an insult. You must make your
own position absolutely plain.

DARWIN
(used to Browne's outbursts & rather amused:)
I'm sorry, my dear Browne, but I'm not sure
which particular insult or new outrage
you have in mind. Surely not Professor Duncan's
lecture on rhubarb?

BROWNE
No, dammit, Darwin. The Plinian Society.
The Plinian Society.

DARWIN
I am bemused, bewildered, and be-baffled.
Enlighten me—and pass me that towel.

Browne takes the towel from the bench, and during next few speeches the towel is flourished in increasingly grotesque oratorical gestures, while Darwin tries to entice it from him.

BROWNE
(after dramatic pause:) They have struck the entire
paper from the record, erased it from the minutes,
completely falsified the account of the meeting.

DARWIN *(surprised but still amused:)*
What? My little paper on the anatomy of
the harmless Flustra Carborea. How peculiarly
melodramatic. Do pass me the towel.

BROWNE
Not *your* paper, Darwin. Mine!

DARWIN
Ah, I see… You must indeed feel outraged.
I agree—it's a positive insult.

BROWNE
It's more than an insult! It's a threat to the very idea
of scientific research, of intellectual freedom, —
of any *progress* in thought.

DARWIN
Surely you exaggerate, my dear insulted friend.
They can't have erased the record.
It simply hasn't been written up yet.
The meeting was only last night, after all. —
Do hand me the towel, old fellow.

BROWNE
I have checked it myself. To see if the summary
was accurate, after that unpleasant row last night.
It was. Oh, yes, it was. Brief and accurate.
"Mr Browne read his paper on: 'The Organisation
of Life and Mind, maintaining that Life is simply the
qualities inherent in the gradually increased
perfection of the organisation of matter and that
Mind is itself material'." Oh yes, they got it very
accurately. Very neatly phrased even.
And very neatly crossed out. In very black ink.
It's damnably outrageous!

Darwin finally secures the towel and sits on the bench drying his hands.

DARWIN
Perhaps it's only a mistake. *(semi-anxious:)*
And is the summary of my paper crossed out also?

BROWNE
Of course it isn't! It's mine they objected to.
Yours didn't threaten their conventional timid
orthodoxies. Mine did.

DARWIN *(mollifyingly)*
Perhaps they weren't sure they had
properly understood your argument —

BROWNE
Don't be so deliberately naive, Darwin.
Of course they understood my argument.
What could be plainer? That Life and Mind

are Material. *That's* the truth they're afraid of.
They've even erased the very *announcement*
of my paper from *last* week's minutes.
Can you call *that* a mistake?

DARWIN *(more serious)*
Yes, I see. What do you intend to do?

BROWNE
I shall protest. I shall demand that the record
be restored. And I want an apology.
I trust that you will support my motion
to that effect at the very next meeting.

DARWIN *(prevaricating)*
Well, I confess, my dear Browne,
I didn't *fully* understand your paper myself.
Of course, I was somewhat tired and distracted
after delivering my own paper—

BROWNE
Darwin, that's not the point! This is a clear case
of the suppression of knowledge, an attack on that
very freedom to propagate unpopular views
which is the crucial condition of scientific research.
Without that, the Pliny Society makes no sense.

DARWIN
Yes, of course. I do agree. But that is partly my
point too. I mean simply that, in my view at least,
—I'm sorry to say—your paper didn't really seem
to be a contribution to *scientific* knowledge, which is,
after all, what the Pliny Society is concerned with.

BROWNE *(furious)*
What!!

DARWIN
I meant, er, perhaps it was considered *inappropriate*,
since it was—as I'm sure you intended—

more a contribution to *philosophical* thought,
a purely *theoretical* speculation, rather than a *scientific*
account. Now, I'm not saying that I won't support
you, but—well, I wouldn't wish you to raise an
unpleasant rumpus concerning Senior Members of
the Society without being absolutely sure of your
grounds—

BROWNE
Darwin!! This just isn't good enough!
You know perfectly well that scientific progress
needs theoretical speculation.

DARWIN
Yes, indeed, of course—but only if it's supported by
evidence, observation, experiment. Your paper,
you must admit, was only a theory —and extremely
interesting — but not clearly based on any hard
evidence, any original and persuasive observations.

BROWNE *(sarcastic)*
Such as your own 'original and persuasive
observations' on the parasitic life of Newhaven
seaweed! Well, we know what happened to those!

DARWIN *(sharply)*
What do you mean? You said my paper had not
been struck from the record.

BROWNE
Oh no, *that's* still there alright. But so too is the
record of the Wernerian Society, three days ago,
at which our most respected teacher, Dr. Grant,
gave a paper drawing the very same conclusions,
from the very same 'original and persuasive
observations', as yourself.

DARWIN *(hurt)*
That is a deeply offensive remark, Browne.
Are you meaning to imply that my paper was

—to put it bluntly— purloined, stolen,
from Dr. Grant's work? I resent your inference.

BROWNE *(appalled)*
Of course not, my dear Darwin, of course not!
On the contrary! My dear fellow, I do apologise.
I meant exactly the opposite. I know and you know
that until three weeks ago the eminent Dr Grant
was arguing precisely the opposite case.
It was *your* observations, *your* conclusions,
that he—to use your blunt word—purloined from
you, not vice versa.

DARWIN *(relieved)*
I'm very glad that that is understood.
I apologise for my unwarranted anger
a moment ago. I thought that you —

BROWNE
No, Charles. But can't you see that it's precisely the
same problem? It's always the professors, the old,
the respected, the eminent authorities, who want to
take the credit for anything new. But equally they
want to suppress the *really* new, the ideas that don't
just dent their prestige a little, but will really
overturn their whole way of thinking. They're afraid
of the new. They're all the same, Grant, Monro, —
and that tedious idiot Duncan above all:
him and his rhubarb!

DARWIN
At least we're agreed about Duncan!
A mind so tightly packed with everything
he's safely known for years that there simply isn't
room for anything new! You should experiment on
Duncan's brain for the next Plinian Society meeting,
as conclusive evidence for your thesis: —
after all, if the mind *is* material, there must come a
point when no new material can be squeezed
into it without some of the old popping out!

I'm sure he'd lend you his brain for a few hours
for demonstration purposes.

BROWNE
Well, he certainly wouldn't miss it.

DARWIN *(serious again)*
But Grant is different, you know. He's befriended
me and, after all, it is *his* specialist field —
or rather beach. He taught me most of what I know
about seaweed—and it would have been, well,
discourteous, to object to his use of my work—

BROWNE
Alright, Charles. All right. But can I definitely
count on you for support at the next meeting?
It's very important.

DARWIN
I agree it's important. But it is only a student society
— and you know how cautious I am.
Perhaps this isn't the right issue.—Yes, yes, my dear
chap. But let me think about it for a day or so.
I do want to be sure in my own mind what the
argument is really about.

BROWNE
The argument is about freedom of thought, Charles.

DARWIN
And about science. May I think about it?

BROWNE
Yes, of course. Think hard about it.

They step off the Platform, and exit together, with Darwin speaking:

The following scene change begins as they walk off, voices still audible:

DARWIN
You know, I caught a sea mouse this morning.
And despite what Turton says, it actually has
four feelers, not two. I counted them myself.

BROWNE
Oh, you're incorrigible, Darwin.

The Platform, with all remaining props, rolls to the rear, out of sight,
The banners fly off, as part of an impressively smooth and visible
scene-change: wing flats with flippers move inwards with painted tree
shapes on both sides; a rear scenery backcloth appears (drop scene
hiding the Platform) with a painting of an idyllic English garden,
based on the 19th c painting of the Wedgwoods at play.

Together the side flats and the rear scenery now form a classic
Restoration stage set.

Lighting: bright September day, late English afternoon,
warm sunshine.,

Dancing onto the stage, as in a frothy musical, a light operetta, or
perhaps a respectable panto, five brightly dressed girls, one of whom is
blindfolded: costumes and general style are a cross between Restoration
gaiety and a BBC Jane Austen production: General giddiness prevails.

[SCENE TWO]

Enter:
SARAH OWEN, FANNY OWEN, EMMA WEDGWOOD,
CHARLOTTE WEDGWOOD, ELIZABETH WEDGWOOD

They are playing blind man's buff. Sarah Owen is 'It'.
Continue briefly till Sarah catches Emma Wedgwood).

SARAH
Caught you!

FANNY
But you have to say who it is.

SARAH
(feels Emma's dress — semi-mockingly:)
My, what rich fabric! Can't be an Owen —
(general laughter) —therefore—a Wedgwood.

FANNY *(sarcastic)*
Brilliant, sister Sarah. It isn't you and it isn't me —
so it must be a Wedgwood. But which one, silly?

SARAH *(feels hair)*
Charlotte—? No, too long. Emma!
It must be Emma!

FANNY
Not so, silly Sarah. Lizbeth has long hair too.

SARAH *(ignores Fanny's taunts)*
It's definitely Emma.

EMMA
Oh dear. Yes, I concede.

(Sarah takes off her blindfold.)

CHARLOTTE
Well done, Sarah!

ELIZABETH *(to Emma)*
Now it's your turn, sister.

FANNY
Or you can suggest a new game instead.
Which is it to be?

EMMA
Can I please have a glass of cordial
—while I decide? I'm terribly hot.

SARAH
Yes, let's all take a rest. I'm quite out of breath.

EMMA *(calls off-stage)*
Daniel.

ELIZABETH
Let's relax anyway — it's far too warm.

Daniel appears: typical shambling elderly servant, comic relief type.

EMMA
Daniel, could we have some cordial please.

Daniel exits, muttering.)

ELIZABETH *(calling after him)*
And some chairs too please Daniel.

CHARLOTTE
When will the men be back?

FANNY
Ah, *men*! It's all cousin Charlotte thinks about these days. Especially that nice Mr. Langton...

CHARLOTTE
It is not!

ELIZABETH
They haven't gone far, only to the first copse.

*From here on, Daniel appears and exits several times,
first with a table for cordial, then cordial and glasses,
then a few chairs, making grumbling heavy weather of it.
Then more chairs.
Conversation continues as the girls take cordial and sit as the chairs
appear. There are never enough chairs.*

EMMA
Charles said he wouldn't stay out long today.

FANNY
But it's the opening day of the season.
Our dear Charles is normally the first in the field
and the last home.

ELIZABETH
Yes, but Charles was anxious to see father
about something important, and wanted to be called
as soon as father returns — so he wouldn't
go too far from the house.

CHARLOTTE
It must be *very* important for Charles to stop
shooting all those lovely fat lazy geese.

SARAH
Pheasants, dear Charlotte, pheasants.

FANNY *(mock-excited)*
It's a proposal! That's what it is.

EMMA
Oh no, it can't be. Not Charles.

FANNY *(teasing)*
And why else should a *young* — *eligible* — *bachelor*
want to speak to *your* father about "something
important." Now, which is it to be?
Emma or Elizabeth?

ELIZABETH
Or Fanny.

(Fanny looks surprised)

EMMA
Not *you*, Fanny. *Our* Fanny.

FANNY

Ah, shame. My heart leapt for just one tiny
moment. *(laughter)*. But it can't be *your* Fanny;
she's far too young. And I rather think it can't be
Elizabeth — a mite too flighty for a future
clergyman *(laughter: Elizabeth is the reverse of this)*
— so it must be Emma. *[to Emma, teasing]*
I think you're 'it' again. It's your lucky day!

SARAH

Do stop, Fanny. We don't even know if it *is*
a proposal, yet, and you're almost sending out
invitations to the wedding.

FANNY

No more games! Here are the men!
Now we'll find out what Charles's little game is.

*Enter, in shooting gear, with guns and bags of shot birds,
speaking as they enter::*

HENSLEIGH WEDGWOOD, LANGTON,
DARWIN, WILLIAM OWEN,

HENSLEIGH

It's an opportunity not to be missed Charles.
Think of the shooting you'll enjoy.
Not mere partridges at any rate.

DARWIN

Hunting English partridges suits me very well,
my dear Hensleigh.

LANGTON

Ah, here are the ladies, awaiting us —

HENSLEIGH
—and kindly equipped with refreshments
for the returning hunters. Good day, cousin Sarah,
cousin Fanny.

FANNY *(mock-flirtatiously)*
Hensleigh, you come bearing gifts
like a true warrior!

HENSLEIGH
Ah, but not *my* gifts, dear Fanny.
You have your brother to thank for three of them
—William - take a bow! — and our excellent
Charles for the remainder.

LANGTON
(mainly aside to Charlotte, a bashful suitor.)
I too must confess my empty-handedness.

Daniel has just appeared with one more chair.

HENSLEIGH
Ah, Daniel. Could we have some cordial
for these thirsty hunters.

EMMA
And bring some more chairs too Daniel.

LANGTON
And could you please take the guns.

HENSLEIGH
Would you also take the birds into the house,,
Daniel.

Daniel, loaded down with guns, bags, birds, trudges off, grumbling.

ELIZABETH *(calling after Daniel)*
And would you tell us if Mr Wedgwood
has returned yet —

FANNY *(calling to Daniel)*
— Mr Darwin is *most* anxious to know.
(directly to Darwin:) And *we* would rather like
to know *why*.

SARAH *(mild reproof.)*
Fanny!

ELIZABETH *(to the men)*
Ignore Fanny's insatiable and impolite curiosity.

CHARLOTTE *(timidly)*
Though we all admit to sharing it...

HENSLEIGH
Have you not told the girls, Charles?

DARWIN
Not yet, Hensleigh. I was going to wait for your
father, but — if the girls would really like to know
—?

FANNY *(laughing)*
Yes, Charles, yes indeed.
We have been speculating madly..

DARWIN
Very well. *(slightly solemn pause)* Two days ago,
I received a rather unexpected proposal..

SARAH *(surprised interruption)*
You have received a proposal —?

DARWIN *(surprised, then laughs)*
I see! Not that kind of proposal, Sarah.

WILLIAM
So that's what all the excitement was about!
My sisters have been match-making again.

DARWIN
I'm so sorry to disappoint you —
if you *are* disappointed..

CHARLOTTE
Deeply, deeply, all of us, Charles.
(Langton looks hurt. Charlotte smiles sweetly at him)

DARWIN
I'm afraid it's a much more mundane proposal —
though romantic and exciting in its own way...

FANNY
Tell us, Charles, tell us!

Darwin begins to pull a letter from his pocket, but is immediately interrupted as:

Enter Daniel, performing the impressive feat of carrying a tray of cordial glasses, two carafes, and two chairs, which he contrives to make look both impossible and some kind of skilled circus act.
Groans from the girls at this badly-timed entrance.
But long-suffering Daniel is used to this kind of treatment.)

ELIZABETH
Has Mr Wedgwood returned yet, Daniel?

DANIEL
Not yet, Miss Elizabeth. *(martyred mode:)*
I shall inform Mr Darwin as soon as he does.

Daniel half exits —

EMMA
There are still not enough chairs, Daniel

DANIEL *(parting shot)*
I do my best, Miss Emma —

ELIZABETH
Thank you, Daniel. Now, Charles —

DARWIN
Well, my dear friends. I shall read you a letter
I received two days ago, from Professor Henslow,
who taught me Natural History at Cambridge.
(reads) "I have been asked by Peacock" *(breaks off:)*
Peacock is Professor of Astronomy. I think.

FANNY
Oh *do* get on with it, Charles.

DARWIN *(reads)*
"..been asked by Peacock to recommend him a
naturalist as companion to Captain Fitzroy,
employed by Government to survey the southern
extremity of America, the territory known as
Tierra del Fuego. Captain Fitzroy wants a man
more as a companion than a mere collector, and
would not take anyone, however good a naturalist,
who was not recommended to him likewise as a
gentleman. Particulars of salary etc., I know
nothing. The ship is *The Beagle*. The voyage is to last
two years, and if you take plenty of books with you,
anything you please may be done. I assure you
I think you are the very man they are in search of.
Your affectionate friend, J.S. Henslow." That's it.

Simultaneous reactions from:

HENSLEIGH: It's a marvellous offer, is it not?
CHARLOTTE: Who is Captain Fitzroy?
FANNY: How long?
ELIZABETH: But whereabouts in South America?
LANGTON: And are you going, sir?
(EMMA *says nothing*)

DARWIN
(answering each of them in turn, rapidly turning to each as appropriate, making a game of it:) Yes indeed it is. /
I have no idea who Captain Fitzroy is. / At least
two years. / Tierra del Fuego. / And, I'm afraid,
my dear Langton, that I really don't know yet.
But: I have already written to Professor Henslow—
(teasing pause) declining his kind offer.

FANNY
Oh. How unromantic.

EMMA *(quietly)*
Why have you decided against, Charles?

WILLIAM
It's an offer I would most certainly be delighted
to take up in your place, Charles.

SARAH
No, brother William, we're not having you
careering off on such a dangerous adventure.

EMMA *(quietly)*
Is that why you're not going, Charles?
— the danger?

DARWIN
No, Emma. I would dearly love to go,
and there would, I believe, be little danger.
But my father has raised a number of sensible
objections and it did not seem right to me to go
against his strongly expressed advice.

WILLIAM
Why on earth does he object, Charles?
It seems a most marvellous chance for you.

DARWIN

He thinks not. *(enumerates, rapidly:)* He regards
the whole scheme as wild and not a little dubious.
The place must first have been offered to many
others, more qualified than myself, and that since
they must have turned down the offer, this must
imply serious doubts as to the vessel, the expedition
or the captain. That it would be disreputable
to my character as a clergyman after I returned.
And he was not convinced that I could actually
do any useful work as a naturalist in the extremely
cramped and uncomfortable conditions of one of
His Majesty's ships. And finally since, in addition
to these objections, my father would be paying
almost all my costs, I really could not easily act
against his advice.

The group is thoroughly deflated by now, as he intended.

HENSLEIGH

But surely it would not cost a very great deal
—and I do think, without any disrespect,
that Dr Darwin could afford to defray your
expenses if the Admiralty would not.

DARWIN

No, father himself did not object to the expense.
It was *I* who raised it, — as a point in *favour* of
the expedition. I said I would have to be
exceedingly clever to over-spend my allowance
on board the Beagle as I did at Cambridge.
He simply replied: "Ah, but they tell me that
you *are* exceedingly clever."

FANNY

Bravo Dr Darwin! *(general laughter)*

DARWIN

(he is playing for effect, knowing what comes next:)

So, I have accordingly posted my reply to Henslow
—and can now see myself settling down to a small
rural parish—with my sermons, and my beetles —

(simultaneously:)

    SARAH: What an anticlimax.
    FANNY: How horribly boring.
    EMMA: So why do you want to see father?

    DARWIN *(enjoying teasing)*
    But: *(pause)* Father then said: *(pause)*
    "If you can find any man of common-sense
    who advises you to go, I will give my consent."
    So — here I am, to consult that man of eminent
    common sense, Mr Josiah Wedgwood,
    my favourite Uncle Josh.

(simultaneously:)

    FANNY: *(cheers)*
    WILLIAM: He will surely advise you to go?
    EMMA: So it's not decided yet?
    HENSLEIGH: Dr Darwin will change his mind
                 if father supports you.

    DARWIN
    I only hope it's not too late to advise Henslow
    if he does. —

Enter Daniel, with another, increasingly bizarre,, chair.
Elizabeth spots him and begins to ask:

    ELIZABETH
    Has father returned yet, Daniel? It is most urgent—

    DANIEL *(overrides her)*
    Mr Wedgwood senior has just returned,
    Miss Elizabeth—and will see Mr Darwin
    in the study immediately.

Daniel gets a round of applause.

FANNY
Wonderful timing, Daniel!

DANIEL *(unabashed by all this)*
I aim to please, Miss Owen.

Daniel starts to exit.

ELIZABETH
Still not enough chairs, Daniel.

DANIEL *(exiting)*
I do my best, ma'am

Darwin gets up, straightens his coat, looks serious.
As Darwin makes an Exit:

(simultaneously:)
HENSLEIGH: Here's your chance, Charles.
LANGTON: Take it with both hands.
WILLIAM: Good luck, Charles
FANNY: Come back as the Great Explorer,Charles
EMMA: *(is silent)*

Darwin exits. The others begin talking, except Emma.

HENSLEIGH
I do hope father tells him to go.
I really think he should.

WILLIAM
It's an absolutely marvellous chance.

CHARLOTTE
I'm not sure. Two years in those horrible jungles,
with snakes and tigers and horrible creepy crawlies.

LANGTON *(quietly, but gauchely)*
They don't have tigers in South America,
dear Charlotte.

HENSLEIGH
No, Charlotte - Charles loves those creepy crawlies,
as you call them. He even ate one once.

(simultaneously:)
FANNY : Yummy!
EMMA: How awful.

HENSLEIGH
He didn't mean to, of course. But while we were at
Cambridge we went out on a field trip, and Charles
had just caught two of his rare beetles. He had one
in each hand, big, black struggling brutes they were.
Suddenly he spots an even rarer third specimen.
In order not to lose any of them he simply popped
one of the beetles he already had into his mouth.

ELIZ & CHARLOTTE: Ugh!
WILLIAM & FANNY : *(laugh)*

HENSLEIGH
Unfortunately, the darn beetle didn't like this
and squirted out some vile fluid into Charles's
mouth. He was so startled that he swallowed the
thing. *But* —he caught the even rarer one and kept
hold of it. That's Charles. He'll be in his element
in South America.

WILLIAM
I do hope Mr Wedgwood advises him to go.
And *I* shall see if there's a place for me
on the ship as well.

SARAH
You're far too young William. And I hope Charles
doesn't go. I'm not sure it will be good for him.

FANNY

Why, Sarah, why? He'd come back with all sorts
of amazing adventure stories. He might become
famous and make his fortune.

EMMA *(interposes firmly)*

I think we should *not* discuss it further,
until father has decided. It would be unfair
both to father and to Charles if they came back
and found us all firmly against whatever decision
they have arrived at.

WILLIAM

But we can't all just sit here in suspense.

EMMA

And we shan't. Since it was my turn to suggest
another game, I propose that we play a round
of 'Musical Chairs'. Come on, everybody up.
I shall sing and you shall all compete.

ELIZABETH

I agree. Come on, arrange the chairs, William.
In a line. Up you get, Fanny.

*William, Langton and Hensleigh quickly arrange chairs. There should
be at least one too few. Emma stands at one side and sings a
sentimental love song or sea shanty (My Bonny Lies Over the Ocean?),
stopping abruptly as necessary while the others play (rapidly).
Charlotte goes out first, then Langton, deliberately, to join her.
They join Emma in singing, harmonising if possible. (Play briefly till:)
Fanny is caught without a chair, so deliberately sits on Hensleigh's lap.*

WILLIAM

That's cheating!

*Enter Josiah Wedgwood and Darwin.
Wedgwood sees Fanny on Hensleigh's lap.*

WEDGWOOD *(amused, teasing)*
Hensleigh, my dear boy! Fanny, I hadn't realised.
You both have my warmest blessings.

HENSLEIGH *(embarrassed)*
It was a game, father.

FANNY
Musical Chairs, Uncle.

WEDGWOOD *(teasing)*
So I see, so I see. These new-fangled games.
Tut, tut. It'll be the end of all decent morality.

WILLIAM
May we ask, sir—

WEDGWOOD
Yes, children, you may. *(pause)* Well, Charles and I
have discussed Dr Darwin's objections thoroughly,
and *(teasing pause)* I am of the opinion that *(pause)*
the offer of a place on the Beagle is *(teasing pause)* —
a very great opportunity, and indeed an honour for
Charles *(Fanny and William cheer)]* and I am to
recommend to the good doctor that he reconsider
his decision and allow Charles to go.

HENSLEIGH
Well done, father!

WILLIAM
Bravo sir!

FANNY *(kisses Darwin's cheek)*
Aren't you pleased, Charles!

WEDGWOOD *(mock reproof)*
Fanny! — have you abandoned
my dearest son so soon?

FANNY
Uncle Josh!

DARWIN
I am delighted to have Uncle Josh's support,
but since it is now extremely urgent to see if
father will indeed change his mind in time for me
to inform Professor Henslow, I must set off
for Shrewsbury immediately.

WEDGWOOD
And since the carriage is still at the door,
we are both leaving at once and I shall speak
to Dr Darwin in person.

DARWIN
I only hope Henslow hasn't yet offered
the place to anyone else.

WEDGWOOD
I am sure we shall get there in time, Charles.
With luck, you can leave for Cambridge yourself
first thing tomorrow morning.

HENSLEIGH
We'll all come and give you a resounding send-off,
Charles.

*General excitement. Triumphant Panto or Nicholas Nickleby type exit
by almost everybody. But Emma exits subdued and silent.*

*Brief pause. Enter Daniel, valiantly carrying about five more
ludicrously miscellaneous chairs. Stops to survey stage,
empty except for scattered chairs, table, and cordial glasses.*

DANIEL
Ah well. I do my best.

Starts to collect chairs, impossibly balancing them. Then gives up.

DANIEL *(whistles to backstage)*
Oi! —Kevin!

The painted backcloth parts or lifts, and the Platform rolls forward fast, empty. Daniel very quickly and skilfully piles all the chairs and props onto it. The Platform with all the gear on it, and Daniel riding it smugly, recedes out of sight as this scene's backcloth disappears and the wing flats recede — to reveal:

Stage Right, almost at right edge of stage: a high Victorian writing desk, facing front, with a narrow bookcase behind it, with several heavy tomes on shelves and lots of folders, files, etc, an oil lamp on the desk. Seated behind the desk, facing front, on a high stool, is EDITOR, in late Victorian gentleman costume. He is writing a manuscript.

Stage Left, almost at left edge of stage : a modern computer desk with a laptop computer, and printer, and elegant modern desk lamp. Seated behind the desk is WRITER, young, contemporary jeans type.)

EDITOR *(speaks across the stage)*
That, young sir, was a *total travesty*.
I *knew* those young ladies. They used to compete among themselves to finish *The Times* crossword first — before breakfast!

WRITER
So — I'm supposed to dramatise the *Times* crossword puzzle?

EDITOR
And I certainly can't recall them ever playing musical chairs, indeed! Or Blind Mans Bluff!

WRITER *(mutters)*
Symbols. Metaphor. Metaphor. Dramatic licence.

EDITOR
Harrumph! And that hideous child in the mask, at the beginning. What was *that* all about?

WRITER

Even Darwin had to be a child sometime, y'know.
He didn't *always* have that long white beard.
I suppose *you* think a man's life begins at 40.
When does life begin? You should know,
you're writing one.

EDITOR

Actually, I am doing the *letters* for now.
I haven't started the life, yet. So don't you start.
Charles had enough trouble with that question
anyway. And that silly bouncing ball. Symbol too,
was it? In my day, cymbals were good old-fashioned
musical instruments, brass band clangers.

WRITER

Er, that was an accident. Sorry.
The stage manager's kid got too excited.

EDITOR

I rather liked the wild duck, though.
Proper Realism.

WRITER

Goose. Barnacle.

EDITOR

I am immune to insults. Look, I have to get on
with my work. Long way to go.

WRITER

So have I — I've got to get him to South America.
Er, any suggestions?

EDITOR

Ah, need my help now, do you. Well, I suppose
you could use this. I've finished with it.
Gone to the printer's already, I'm happy to say.

Writer crosses the stage to get a manuscript letter from Editor
and reads it out loud as he returns to his place:)

WRITER *(reads)*
"My Dear Sisters, We sailed, as you know,
on the 27th December and have been fortunate
enough to have had a fair and moderate breeze.
In the Bay of Biscay there was a long and
continuous swell, and the misery I endured from
sea-sickness is far beyond what I ever guessed at.
The real misery only begins when you are so
exhausted that even a little exertion makes a feeling
of faintness come on — *(skips a bit)* — I find to my
great surprise that a ship is singularly comfortable
for all sorts of work. Everything is so close to hand,
and being cramped makes one so methodical that
in the end I have been a gainer. If it were not for
sea-sickness, the whole world would be sailors.
We are now setting sail for Fernando Noronha,
off the coast of Brazil.."

During this reading, the great ship Beagle moves slowly into view,
moving across the stage from SR towards SL, into playing position.
If possible, show the whole ship, side-on, brow to stern, but only in a
painted 2-D form, like a toy cut-out, and out of proportion to human
figures. The broad-side, facing the audience, is at least the height of a
tall man. Very theatrical, brightly coloured, almost Peter Pan or
Sinbad, but fairly accurate details. If possible, artificial waves are
moving up and down at its base.

The rear scenery now shows a painted panorama of a
South American location :Port Desire.

EDITOR *(looking scornfully at ship)*
And what's this, then? *Melo-drama*?!
How positively vulgar.

WRITER
Your period, not mine. Can I have another letter?

EDITOR
Vowel or consonant?

WRITER
Very droll.

EDITOR
You don't want to read out the whole volume,
do you?

WRITER
No, one more will do —
just while they finish getting the set ready.

*Goes and gets a second letter, and reads it aloud as the ship reaches its
playing position and Captain Fitzroy appears on deck.*

WRITER *(reads aloud:)*
"My dear Henslow, One great source of perplexity
to me in this new world is an utter ignorance
whether I note the right facts, and whether they are
of sufficient importance to interest others — *(skims)*
— I took several specimens of an Octopus which
possessed a most marvellous power of changing its
colours, equalling any chameleon, and evidently
accommodating the changes to the colour of the
ground which it passed over. The fact appears to be
new, as far as I can find out —*(skims quickly)*—
There is a most important error in the longitude of
South America, to settle which this second trip has
been undertaken. The Captain continues very kind
and does everything in his power to assist me.
I never in my life met with a man who could endure
so great a share of fatigue. He works incessantly,
and when apparently not employed, is thinking.
If he does not kill himself, he will during this voyage
do a wonderful quantity of work."
*(breaks off reading, looks up to the Fitzroy actor
and addresses him directly:)*

That's your cue, I take it. Ready yet?
(Fitzroy nods) Action!

                EDITOR *(mutters)*
Hardly.

As [SCENE THREE] begins, Writer returns to his desk and sits.
Editor and Writer remain visible throughout,
though their respective lamps are subdued.

Writer watches the scene and takes occasional notes.
Editor works diligently at a manuscript.

This scene is to be acted just on the edge of a parody of mid-Victorian
Melodrama conventions.

Fitzroy is now joined on the upper deck by Darwin,
both looking tired and sweaty.

                FITZROY
Darwin, there you are. I was told you had returned
early. I confess I was most surprised.
I thought you would have enjoyed your trip up-
country with Lennon. But you have arrived just in
time for us to lunch together. Will you join me?

                DARWIN
(He is tired, dispirited, flat; underneath is a weary anger.)
Thank you, Fitzroy. No, if you'll excuse me.
I need to breathe some good sea-breezes for a
while.

                FITZROY
Well, I shall at least take some refreshment with
you. I have been calculating charts all morning,
and the cabin is rather too warm for comfort.
(Fitzroy calls down into the ship:) Jemmy —
Would you oblige us with some refreshment.

(to Darwin) You were perhaps fatigued by the heat and the travel? The forest can be extremely tiring.

DARWIN

No, the journey itself was a delight. I was enthralled, enraptured by the forest. Its great spaces and curious warm silences, the creepers entwining the sunlight, the sense of vitality, of everything so incredibly alive. No, Nature is at her most impressive and fascinating for me here. I regret that it was the *men* who fatigued—and angered—me.

FITZROY

Angered? I thought Lennon a very decent man — not quite a gentleman, of course, but a solidly respectable planter. Did you not get along together?

DARWIN

Well, there was an extremely unpleasant quarrel. Pistols were drawn.

FITZROY *(interrupts)*
Good Lord, I hope..

A fairly large aperture silently opens in the broad-side of the Beagle, showing a near life-size Victorian Toy Theatre: framed in view is a well-lit tableau from a melodrama, with highly coloured cut-outs of two men confronting each other, with pistols dramatically drawn, their poses taken from Skelt's model theatre figures.

The following Toy Theatre scenes could be done as animated cut-outs or as back-projected 19th c print illustrations.
One is melodrama, one is gauzed, one is shadow theatre.

DARWIN

No, Fitzroy, not myself and Lennon.
I intervened to prevent any actual bloodshed.
It was between Lennon and his manager—.

FITZROY

Cowper. Yes, I have met him. An irascible type.
And Lennon is Irish, too, of course. A volatile
mixture. The heat doesn't help tempers out here.

The Toy Theatre curtains close on the inset scene.

DARWIN

It wasn't the quarrel itself. It was what Lennon
threatened to do that sickened and angered me.
He threatened to sell off all his women and children
slaves, to take them to Bahia and auction them off
— separately from their husbands and menfolk.
It was disgusting, abominable.

FITZROY

I don't follow you, Darwin.
What had this to do with Cowper? Or you?

DARWIN

Cowper had fathered a mulatto child upon one
of Lennon's female slaves—a child of whom
he is extremely fond. This was Lennon's way of
insulting Cowper. Not only selling off his child
but reminding him that his son was a mere slave
like all the others, absolutely in Lennon's power.

FITZROY

It seems a mean-minded sort of trick, I grant you.
But Cowper could then have bought the child
himself if he so badly wanted it.

DARWIN

To buy one's own son!! But it wasn't only Cowper
I was thinking of. In a mere fit of pique, Lennon
could break up dozens of families and sell them off
like so many oranges. It was appalling.

Jemmy Button appears on deck with refreshment drinks,
serves them silently, exits.

FITZROY *(paternally)*
My dear Darwin, I realise your feelings are
likely to be quite strong on the subject of slavery.
You haven't lived with it, or seen it very often,
as I have.

DARWIN
I have seen enough of it recently, Fitzroy.
We stopped on the way up-river for refreshments.
A little slave boy, six or seven years old, handed me
a glass of water. There was a small speck of dirt
on the glass. And for that his master beat the boy
around the head with a horsewhip, three times,
before I could stop him.

*Toy Theatre curtains open: behind gauze this time: a child being
whipped by master, as in the incident described.*

FITZROY
You really shouldn't have stopped him, you know.
The authority of the slave-owner is absolute here,
and should *not* be interfered with. Without such
discipline and punishment it would be quite
impossible to keep control over the slave
population—and we would, I'm afraid,
have another Haiti uprising on our hands.
Besides, even a mere speck of dirt
in this country could cause sickness or fever.
The master was quite right to chastise.

Toy Theatre: scene closes.

DARWIN
It was the master that sickened me, not the water —
morally sickened me. I realised how little I still
understood. *(bitterly:)* In Rio, that ageing contessa
who lived opposite our lodgings showed me—
during afternoon tea! —the thumbscrews she kept
to 'discipline' her house-slaves. I nodded politely,

and examined them with a mild interest, thinking
them a kind of curio that she never actually used,
but merely kept as a threat. Then, on Lennon's
estate, I actually heard thumbscrews being used
on a slave. I heard the screams from the river
even before we landed. They were shattering,
howls of sheer agony. And I was told that
thumbscrews were 'normal practice'
(very bitter)—to keep the servants in their place.

*Toy Theatre shows a silent scene, with the cut-out shadow silhouette
of a slave being tortured with thumbscrews.*

FITZROY
You over-react, Darwin. I agree such suffering
is *most* distressing. But it is not the institution of
slavery you should blame. It is the unfortunate
inheritance of this vicious country. It was the
Spaniards and the Portuguese who colonised
most of this continent, and they brought with them
the abominable practices of their corrupted church.
Those thumbscrews come from the Catholic
Inquisition, not from slavery itself.

Toy Theatre scene fades into darkness. Curtains close.

DARWIN
Well, I agree about the Portuguese at any rate.
I can never see any of that diminutive, arrogant
race, with their murderous countenances,
without almost wishing for Brazil to follow the
example of Haiti.

FITZROY
That is going rather *too* far.

DARWIN
Perhaps not far enough, Fitzroy. Perhaps the
Indians should revolt as well as the slaves.

In one evening in General Rosas' camp,
I saw over a hundred Indian prisoners brought in.
By next morning they had all been hanged or shot
— except, of course, the more attractive of the
Indian women. All over that area, there were
dozens of skeletons dangling from the trees.
The vultures had learned to hover over the
General's encampment. *(flat, depressed pause)*
It truly is a savage world.

    FITZROY
(He puts his hand briefly on Darwin's shoulder)
Come, Darwin, I haven't often seen you
so depressed. Remember that we will soon
do our own small bit to civilise this savagery.
(gets enthusiastic:) We can at last make sail for
Tierra del Fuego. And I shall begin my own
experiment in Christianising this continent.
We shall land Jemmy Button and his family,
and we will soon see the effect of their
Christian conversion upon their fellow natives.
I have the *highest* hopes that, under God's
Providence, in a few years there will be a
thriving Protestant outpost amongst the Fuegians.
Now, does that not console you, Darwin?

    DARWIN *(still depressed)*
I trust you are right, Fitzroy.

    FITZROY
Jemmy once told me, Darwin, that during the
severest winters in his own bleak and icy land,
the men would kill the old women and eat them.
But they would keep the dogs, because at least
the dogs were trained to catch otters for them.
A tribe that makes *that* choice is even worse
than any slave-owning Portuguese.

DARWIN

Perhaps, Fitzroy. But I am not quite so sanguine
as to the effects of Jemmy's newly-acquired
Christianity upon the rest of his tribe.
(sudden anger:) Do you know what really sickened me
about Lennon. The morning after the quarrel,
when he had spent half the night planning to sell
these women and children like cattle—
the following morning was a Sunday, and he
assembled all the slaves in the compound,
for a religious service. After the prayers and the
hymns, he solemnly blessed them all in the name of
God—and sent them off to work. That blessing
stuck in my gorge. It was hypocritical, obscene.
Immediately after the service I asked for a guide
and set off to return here.

FITZROY

I disagree profoundly, Darwin. It is precisely
such a service that should have made you glad.
Without that moment of shared worship
and God's blessing, would not Lennon be in danger
of entirely forgetting that for those slaves he is the
representative of a Christian civilisation,
and should act accordingly.

DARWIN *(sarcastically)*

Precisely.

FITZROY

Darwin, you are too bitter. The conditions of those
slaves are not as bad as you imagine. I have seen
them at close quarters, and they are truly just
as good as those of our own agricultural labourers
in England —

DARWIN *(interrupts, angry)*

—whom you may remember, sir, revolted against
those very conditions just two years ago.

FITZROY *(getting angry)*
That was the regrettable excitement and false
expectations aroused by that unfortunate Reform
Act. If you had ever had to manage a large estate,
you would know that it is impossible to devise any
really radical improvements for the estate workers.
It is in the nature of their work to be difficult and
harsh. And the same applies to the plantations here.

DARWIN
Yet we can put so much ingenuity, expense and
effort into continually improving our very breeds
of cattle and sheep for our own benefit —
while we proclaim that the conditions of the men
who tend those sheep and cattle are 'incapable of
radical improvement'.

FITZROY *(extremely angry)*
I knew I had invited a Whig on board, but not a
Radical Chartist. You have deceived me, sir.

DARWIN
I am not a Chartist, Fitzroy, but my family has been
in the forefront of the campaign against slavery
since the time of my grandfather, and you cannot
expect me to tolerate an institution I regard as evil
—and unchristian too, sir.

FITZROY
The Bible has nothing to say against slavery,
Darwin. It is Christianity which makes us truly free,
whether citizen or slave, as St Paul himself says.
I deeply believe that, Darwin. *(more conciliatory, softer
tone:)* Look, my dear Darwin, I am not inhumane.
I too have been concerned about the condition
of the slaves in this country. When I first visited
Lennon's own plantation, I made a point of asking
his slaves outright if they were content, if they
would prefer to be free upon the open market,
and to a man they replied that they would not.

DARWIN
I somehow doubt if that is enough, Fitzroy.
(longish pause) Allow me to show you something.
It was a farewell gift from one of my cousins,
Emma Wedgwood. Her grandfather, the Josiah
Wedgwood who founded the potteries, produced
hundreds of these pottery medallions, and Emma
gave me one as a keepsake. Read the inscription.

*Darwin hands the medallion, which he has had on a chain round his
neck, to Fitzroy.*

*In the Toy Theatre aperture is projected a large-scale medallion,
of a slave in chains, the famous image, with the motto legible.*

FITZROY *(turning the medallion in his hand)*
"Am I not a man and a brother."

DARWIN
And are they not men and our brothers, women and
our sisters? Would you tolerate your own brother
or sister living under these conditions? *(pause, then
quietly:)* May I ask if Lennon was present when you
asked his slaves whether they would rather be free?

FITZROY
He was indeed.

DARWIN
And what is the answer of a slave worth
when his absolute master is present to hear him?

FITZROY *(very angry indeed)*
Sir, do you doubt my word as a gentleman?
(icy pause) I might perhaps remind you, sir, that while
your Mr Josiah Wedgwood was busily campaigning
to free the slaves from the estates of the landed
gentry, he was equally busily perfecting that
abominable system of so-called factory manufacture

which makes the condition of our agricultural
labourers seem a positive paradise by comparison.
(pause, still angry) Again, I ask you, sir,
do you doubt my word as a gentleman?

DARWIN *(wearily)*
No, Fitzroy, no. I apologise. Perhaps it is
simply that I am beginning to doubt
the word of an entire civilisation.

Writer abruptly steps into centre of stage and interrupts the scene:

WRITER
Er, sorry, could we just stop it there, please.

Actors look at him, but then relax, as if in rehearsal:

FITZROY *(as actor)*
You mean to hold it, as a *tableau*
—or a freeze-frame?

WRITER
A freeze-what?

EDITOR *(supercilious)*
I believe it's a kinematic term, dear boy.
I thought you would have invented moving pictures
by now? Would have worked a lot better
than those pathetic toy theatre contraptions.
Could have had the whole ship in real motion, too.

WRITER
And I thought you were a historian, not a media
prophet. You're supposed to be editing Darwin's
letters, not *Pirates of the Caribbean*. Get back to work,
please. I'm relying on you.

EDITOR
I only asked. I was looking at those *tableaux* scenes
and thought: move them about a bit, have the lights

flicker on and off rapidly, and you've got a quite
interesting effect. I heard some chappie did
something similar with photo-graphics.
We could pre-invent Kinema you know.

WRITER
I'm a theatre man, I never go to the kinema.
Can we just go back to the scene.

EDITOR
Why, what's the problem?

WRITER
Do we know—do *you* know—
whatever happened to Jemmy Button?

EDITOR
Ah, I'm was just coming to that.
Here, somewhere. Sad, really.

*Editor fishes out a letter. Writer goes across and gets it. Reads it out,
direct to the audience, while, unobtrusively, the Toy Theatre curtains
close, the aperture closes up, and the ship is now whole again.*

WRITER *(reads)*
"My dear sisters, East Falkland Islands, April 1834.
After visiting some of the southern islands, we came
through the magnificent scenery to Jemmy Button's
own country, to see what had happened to Captain
Fitzroy's mission of last year. — We could hardly
recognise poor Jemmy. Instead of the clean, well-
dressed stout lad we left last year, we found a naked,
thin, squalid savage. — The other converted
Fuegians had moved away to their own territory
some months ago, having stolen all Jemmy's
clothes. Now he had nothing except a bit of blanket
round his waist. —The Captain offered to take him
back to England, but this, to our surprise, he at
once refused.

In the evening his young wife came alongside
and *that* showed us the reason. Jemmy was quite
contented. —Last year, in the height of his
indignation, he said his fellow countrymen were
'people no *sabe [know]* nothing—damned fools.'
Now they were 'very good people', with too much
to eat and all the luxuries of life. Jemmy and his wife
paddled away in their canoe, loaded with presents
and very happy." *(finishes reading)* Interesting. *(to
Editor:)* Got anything else on the Falklands?

                    EDITOR
It'll be in the edition. No more letters, *please*.
You're just using all my hard work.
And what do I get out of it?

                    WRITER
I can give you a computer if you like
—make the work easier.

                    EDITOR
I already know how to count, thank you.
And if you mean Mr Babbage's Difference Engine,
I spoke to my printer—and he couldn't make the
contraption work at all.

                    WRITER
OK, something simpler. Props!

The Props man walks on carrying a typewriter, old fashioned, bulky.

                    PROPS
This do?

                    WRITER
That'll do nicely, thank you.

Props exits.
Writer takes the typewriter across the stage and presents it to Editor.

EDITOR
What's this new-fangled machine?

WRITER
The patent for typewriters was registered in 1714.
Hardly 'new-fangled'.

EDITOR
You expect me to acquire transferable skills
at my time of life? *(looks at typewriter)*
It won't catch on. *(looks at keyboard)*
Q.W.E.R.T.Y —what's the sense in that?

WRITER
It's so that your ribbon doesn't stick.

EDITOR
I don't wear ribbons in my hair. I give up.
Time to adapt, I suppose. *(he taps at a key or two
tentatively, then quickly begins typing fluently, but silently.)*
Do carry on. But can we please cut out the theatre
gimmicks.

WRITER
Alright, we'll do the moonlight scene.
(to actors, who go back into role:) OK? Ready?

[SCENE FOUR]

Lighting changes to beautiful blue moonlight. Peaceful.
Backcloth has changed to a different panorama.
(Valparaiso, or open sea.)
Darwin is leaning pensively over the ship's rail.
Fitzroy stands looking out.
Friendly relaxed relation between them.
A quiet conversation begins.
Avoid too much parody.

FITZROY *(kindly)*
Homesick, lovesick, or seasick?

DARWIN
Not sick at all, Fitzroy. Thinking.

FITZROY
That's a kind of sickness, my dear Darwin. And
what fever have your thoughts caught this evening?

DARWIN
The sea. Always the sea.
The marvellous immensity of it.

FITZROY
"Water, water, everywhere" eh? —
Provided, that is, you forget all those islands
and reefs we've been so meticulously charting.
The poet's Ancient Mariner didn't sail aboard
a surveying ship, that's for certain.

DARWIN
Yes, indeed.—Though Coleridge was right,
you know. That sheer weight of water.
Always moving. It still staggers me every time
I really look at it. Immense. Immeasurable.

FITZROY
Immeasurable? Let us hope not.
Or my task would be singularly futile.

DARWIN
Forgive my romantic inexactitude, Fitzroy.
I'm afraid it's the hidden sentimentalist
beneath the hard geologist! Though my thoughts
are still those of a rather puzzled geologist,
even in my present mood, of relaxed indulgence.

FITZROY

I thought so. My dear Darwin, in nearly three years,
I have never seen you completely relaxed.
You're always either working —or seasick.
So what puzzles you tonight?

DARWIN

Time. Energy. The sheer forces of nature. *(pause])*
When I was a child, our home overlooked the
River Severn at Shrewsbury, and I still remember
the stone steps down to the river, near the bridge —
how the river had gradually worn away the lowest
steps, so that they were absolutely smooth and very
slippery. My father had to save me once from
sliding in. But the steps which were out of reach
of the river were hard, square-edged, definite.
They seemed made of a different substance
altogether. *(pause)* And now I'm trying in my mind
to multiply that effect a thousand, thousand times.
I'm thinking of those great sweeping bays,
 all along this coastline, worn away so smoothly
for hundreds of miles.

FITZROY

I at least am grateful for the erosion.
Those bays are extremely easy to map.

DARWIN

But it makes my work much harder.
Do you remember those fossils I found,
at Port Saint Julian and Punta Alta?

FITZROY

Remember them! They still give me nightmares —
the *monsters* you conjured up from them!
What was it at Port St Julian — a cross between
a camel, a giraffe and an anteater?

DARWIN *(laughs)*
That was only my incompetent attempt
to draw one for you. It was a Macrauchenia,
not a monster. A perfectly sensible brute
in its own terms — and in its own time.

FITZROY
Well, I'm heartily glad it was left out of the ark.
As one captain to another, Noah would have had
my deepest sympathy if he'd had *that* aboard
in the flesh. Even its bones were bad enough.

DARWIN
Well, I shall have very few bones to inconvenience
you with on this coast, thanks to the sea.
There's almost no fossil record at all —
and that's what puzzles me. There ought to be —
though the land has clearly been raised several
hundreds, perhaps even thousands, of feet —

FITZROY *(interrupts)*
I beg your pardon, Darwin. Did you say *raised*
several thousand feet? — In what sense?

DARWIN
(pause) Quite literally.

FITZROY
That hardly helps.

DARWIN
Well, I rather hesitate to explain.
I've been puzzling about it myself for nearly six
months. *(another pause, then plunges:)*
On my expedition up the Andes, I came across
something quite extraordinary. *(hesitates, then
continues:)* At the very peak of one mountainous
climb, I was some 12,000 feet above sea-level,
perched on a windy crag of rock —a stupendous
view below me —behind me a superb chaos

of high mountains —above me only the thin sky and the great wheeling condors. The solitude and the splendour were quite overwhelming — like hearing a chorus of the Messiah in full orchestra —

FITZROY *(coughs ironically)*
That suppressed Romantic is emerging again —

DARWIN *(laughs briefly)*
Well, it was the hard-nosed geologist who received a shock. As I looked down at the bare red rock on which I stood, I suddenly saw a perfect fossil bed —but not the bones of some great extinct bird, or a high-flying condor. There, twelve thousand feet *above* the sea — was a bed of *sea-shells*.
Then, as I began to explore in a kind of frantic amazement, I found a veritable forest of petrified *pine-trees* — with *marine* rock deposits, still clinging to them. Such trees, Fitzroy, are now found only on the *Atlantic* coast—which was 700 miles distant from me and 12,000 feet below me.
That rock on which I stood, amid those great-winged wheeling condors, had once been *beneath the ocean*, several hundred miles to the east. I tell you, Fitzroy, that rock seemed to tremble beneath me — and the whole world with it.

FITZROY *(pause; then, elated:)*
I can quite understand your excitement, Darwin — and I warmly congratulate you sir. It's an almost miraculous discovery —*(Fitzroy enthusiastically shakes Darwin's hand)* — and I am deeply proud that this magnificent find should have been made on the voyage of the Beagle.

DARWIN *(releases hand limply)*
But, Fitzroy, I don't understand your elation —

FITZROY *(still excited, but puzzled)*
But surely, Darwin, you can see the tremendous
significance of your discovery. Does this not
demonstrate, *demonstrate*, that —as the Bible says—
the Flood did indeed cover the very highest places
of the earth, even the Andes themselves!

DARWIN
I see. *(flat, pause)* No, Fitzroy, I'm afraid I don't
believe that my fossilised sea-shells demonstrate
that at all. On the contrary. I said that the *land*
had been raised several thousand feet, not the sea.

FITZROY
But that's preposterous Darwin!!
It's a ludicrous idea! We know that the sea
can rise to cover the land, but surely not —

DARWIN
—And we also know that the land can rise
out of the sea, Fitzroy. After the earthquake
at Conception I showed you myself how
the rock-strata had split and shifted upward ...

FITZROY
Yes, but a mere five or six feet.
Not twelve thousand!

DARWIN
That was only one earthquake, Fitzroy —
and in just five or six seconds it destroyed that
entire town. The shockwaves damaged villages
four hundred miles away. Just think of the
immense force at work which could do that.
So, could not a *thousand* earthquakes have raised
the earth's surface again and again and again.

FITZROY

Nature does not work like a small boy
with a hammer: Bang! Bang! Bang! -
And to raise a whole *continent* by earthquakes!?

DARWIN

Not only earthquakes, Fitzroy. That's what
I have been thinking about. Three months ago,
we both stood on this very deck and watched the
whole sky and the sea blazing with light
from the fires of the Osorno volcano.
That eruption was one hundred miles inland.
Imagine, remember, the tremendous power,
the heat, the immeasurable energies released
in that eruption. You ask about a whole continent.
When we docked at Valparaiso, I read all the
newspaper accounts of that eruption.
On that very same night, volcanoes erupted
all along this coast, from Anoncagua to Cosequina
— That's over three thousand miles. An eruption
on a gigantic scale, *an explosion 3,000 miles long.*
Can you feel the continent moving, Fitzroy?

FITZROY

No, I most certainly cannot, Darwin.
Such wild speculations are close to insanity —
and any sane man, let alone a man of Christian faith,
must surely prefer the Bible's account of a Flood
to this — this incredible notion. The world you
conjure up smacks more of Milton's hell
than of the good earth God made for us.

DARWIN

A good earth that boils over into molten lava,
burning, burying those dead and dying people
in Conception, an earth that bucks and trembles,
demolishing the six-foot thick walls of the very
cathedral at Conception

FITZROY
That remark is close to blasphemy, Darwin.

DARWIN
I am sorry. It was not intended as such. —
I am simply trying to understand these
extraordinary phenomena, to see if volcanoes,
earthquakes, fossilised sea-shells on a mountain
peak, and the immense force of the sea itself are
linked. I am trying to grasp what the effect of
such forces acting, constantly, repeatedly, over a
long period would — could — be. If the sea can
so wear away the land, how much has it worn away?
And for how long? If a single earthquake can lift
the level of an entire town, what could a thousand
earthquakes do? And what time-scale would be
needed? How old is the sea itself? *(slight pause,
excited:)* Fitzroy, how long is this ship?

FITZROY *(taken aback)*
I beg your pardon.

DARWIN
How long is the Beagle, from prow to stern?

FITZROY *(wary)*
Ninety feet.

DARWIN
Ninety feet. *(does mental calculation)*
Look at them, Fitzroy. Ninety feet.
If those ninety feet represented one million years
do you know how long a hundred years would be?

FITZROY *(baffled)*
A foot, six inches —

DARWIN
One-tenth of an inch.
(uses his finger and thumb on the rail to demonstrate)

That would be one hundred years. And we know there have been *ten* such earthquakes just in the last hundred years. Now, look again, at the length of the ship. One million years. A million years of those incredible forces at work. And perhaps a million years of men and women dying in earthquakes, volcanic eruptions. It is almost unthinkable. But then imagine a ship *three thousand feet long. (pause)* And now look at the sea.

FITZROY
Darwin, you positively frighten me. I fear for your soul. A man who has talked as you have done leaves no room for God. Is not His power more inconceivably immense than these vast forces you speak of? Is not His action more intelligible than these blind eruptions and explosions that so fascinate you. Are you not afraid of losing sight of the Creator himself in all this talk of terrible powers and incredible times? Are you not forgetting that it is God who *created* the land and the sea, the mountains and the rivers, the condors and the sea-shells too. And created you also.

DARWIN *(suddenly tired and very flat)*
Yes, Fitzroy. Yes. *(pause, then slowly:)*
May I tell you a story about one of my teachers at Cambridge? Professor Sedgwick. I once approached him with news that greatly excited me. I had been talking to a labourer near my home in Shrewsbury, and had made clear to him my interest in rocks, fossils, shells, and the like. He had offered to fetch me an unusual shell which he said he had found deeply buried in a gravel-pit nearby, where he worked. *(pause).* When I saw the shell I immediately recognised it as a *tropical* volute shell, not to be found naturally within a thousand miles of England.

This seemed to me a find of very considerable importance. *(pause)* But when I explained the circumstances to Professor Sedgwick, expecting an excited response, he merely said that he thought and *hoped* that the shell had been recently *thrown* there by someone—and that if it were truly embedded and somehow *naturally* deposited there—a tropical shell in the middle of England—then the find would be the greatest *misfortune* for geological science. *(slight pause)* I was astonished. Why should such an amazing find be a *mis*fortune for geology? Because —Sedgwick explained—it would overthrow all that we thought we knew about the surface deposits of the Midland Counties, and that since science consists in *grouping* facts so that *general* laws or conclusions might be drawn from them, this *single* shell would simply disperse the existing groupings, break down the available laws, yet of itself provide no new groupings, no viable general conclusions. *(longish pause)* Perhaps you can now see why, as a scientist, I am puzzled, and even dismayed, by those shells I found upon the Andes.

FITZROY *(hesitates quite a long time)*
I think we both need some sleep. I have found this conversation painful as well as tiring. And I intend to do my best to forget it. I strongly suggest that you also forget these thoughts. *(pause; quite kindly:)* I shall wish you good night, Darwin. *(pause)* And may God bless and keep you.

DARWIN *(flat)*
Good night, Fitzroy. Thank you.

Fitzroy descends. Darwin remains, looking again at the sea. Pause.

DARWIN
(to himself, quietly, but audibly)
How old is the sea? *(pause)*
How long is the soul?

Moonlight fades to black. Beagle in darkness.

The lamps on the two side desks slowly come up,
the only pools of light. Allow a pause.

EDITOR
So, now you've established that there's
been quite a long time since the creation.
My word, you took your time about it!
In fact, too many words—and *my* words too—
from *my* edition. I thought Charles became
famous not for geology but for biology—
or am I just wasting my time here?

WRITER
Well, it took him a long time to get there.
And without a long time for the earth
to have been around, there wouldn't have been
time enough for his biology. He couldn't have fitted
the theory of evolution in, if creation was only
six thousand years ago.

EDITOR
Slow worker was he?

WRITER
Well, not *that* slow. He had his basic idea within
eighteen months of coming home from the voyage.
But how do you ever *really* arrive at a *new* idea?

EDITOR
Me? Comes natural. Selection. Breeding.
Aristocracy of fine minds. Intellectual inheritance.
Oxbridge education. Bred in tooth and claw.

All pretty obvious, really. None of this laborious
pounding away at a damn typewriter, I can tell you.

WRITER
But the notion of the survival of the fattest,
how did he ever arrive at that?

EDITOR
Er, he didn't. Misprint. First printing only.
Managed to get it corrected. *Fittest.*

WRITER
Oh. I was looking forward to writing that scene.

EDITOR
Typing error. Thanks to you. Call it a character
mutation if you like. A slip of the font.

WRITER
Pity. I could have propagated a whole new drama
from that misprint. 'The Victory of the Obese:
a Rolling Epic.' Fat cheque too.

EDITOR
You're just winging it, aren't you—flying blind?

WRITER
Ahah! Another anachronism, eh?
So how do you know about aeroplanes?

EDITOR
What's anachronistic about a bat? You just don't
know where you're going, or how to get there.

WRITER
Nothing new in that. It's how Nature operates.

EDITOR
I'm not having Mother Nature operate on me.
Far too painful.

WRITER
It's a cruel business, writing. I think it's time for
a touch of Artaud.

EDITOR
Our toe??

WRITER
Theatre of Cruelty. All the rage, once.

EDITOR
The Roman amphitheatre? Gladiator shows? Wild
animals tearing the critics apart, that kind of thing?

WRITER
That's later in the show. I was referring to
a French drama theorist.

EDITOR
Might have known.

WRITER
Keep typing. You're in this scene.
You can have a break after it.

[SCENE FIVE]

*This scene is (like) a nightmare. Compare Eliot's Becket surrounded
by the Tempters, or Maxwell Davies, Eight Songs for a Mad King —
Most of the voices, except Darwin's, could be orchestrated on a
pre-recording, with FX, and mimed to by the Characters if necessary.
The numbers identifying the passages are for convenience only,
and not to be spoken.*

*Editor and Writer desks are faintly lit.
Editor begins typing away, very audibly.
Writer begins to do so also, with his printer rapidly printing out
the results. Single pages fluttering to the ground.*

Sound effects: The Bali Monkey Chant begins to be audible.
It grows in crescendo during the scene. And gradually is joined by the
increasing sound of lots of typewriters.

The only light on the Beagle is a dim spot on the Toy Theatre aperture,
now open. And through the aperture walks Darwin.
He stands centre stage. Darwin speaks:
(These are quotations from his journals and working notes.)

> DARWIN
> [1.] The mind thinks with extraordinary rapidity.
> It is solely the comparison with past ideas which
> makes consciousness and which tells one of reality.
>
> [2.] Perhaps one cause of the intense labour of
> original inventive thought is that none of the ideas
> are habitual, nor recalled by obvious associations,
> as by reading a book.

As Darwin speaks, the Characters emerge from the open aperture of
the Toy Theatre behind him.
The Characters are dressed in variations of the costumes seen in
previous scenes, perhaps with a suggestion of skeletal overlays,
as in the Kangaroo Dance. They wear a variety of animal masks.
Suggestion of a Greek Chorus going insane (Artaud, Living Theater)

They circle, like dancers in the Kangaroo Dance, around Darwin,
and grab pages from either the Editor or the Writer,
chanting, screaming, shouting or hissing the passages (on the pages)
directly at Darwin, as they circle with increasing menace.

After reading out their pages, they just scatter them on the floor.
Much ritual stamping of feet. Drumming. Strobes.
Working towards a general crescendo of cacophony.

Throughout, on tape, several voices from previous scenes are heard
as below, in interplay with the passages 'spoken' by the Characters,
whose voices are themselves overlapping and simultaneous.

Vary the recorded order, repeat, add, and distort, as necessary:

FITZROY: That's a kind of sickness, Darwin.

BLACKIE: I don't know where I really came from, where I really came from —

FITZROY: He could have bought the child himself if he so badly wanted it —

BROWNE: What could be plainer. That life and mind are material. They understood!

FITZROY: The men would kill the old women and eat them. —

EMMA: Is that why you're not going Charles— the danger?

FITZROY: The monsters you conjured up from them. —

FANNY: Come back as the great explorer Charles

FITZROY: Am I not a man and a brother —

FITZROY: Nature doesn't work like a small boy with a hammer: bang bang bang!

Two Characters simultaneously, or overlapping, as they attack Darwin:

[3.] The possibility of *two quite different trains of thought going on in the mind* may really explain what habit is. The habitual individual remembers things done in the other habitual state. In the habitual train of thought, one idea simply calls up another and so the consciousness is *not* awakened.

[4.] There may be *two or three trains of thought at once.* In sleep only *one* idea is awake. When one is *awake, many* necessarily are. When one is deeply reasoning,

a crowd of other trains of thought are in progress.
Therefore works of imagination are *hard work.*
Though *dreams* do that.

Three Characters simultaneously, or overlapping:

[5.] Animals that we have made our *slaves,*
we do not like to consider our *equals.*
*Do not slave owners wish to make the black man an other
species.* If we let conjecture run wild, then animals
our *fellow brethren* in pain, disease, death & suffering,
our slaves in the most laborious work,
our companions in our amusements.

[6.] *Extraordinary curiosity of monkeys.*
Dr Smith says every baboon & monkey
that ever he saw knew women: he has repeatedly
seen them try to pull up petticoats
and if women not afraid clasp them round waist.

[7.] From our origin in *one common ancestor*
we may *all* be netted together. I saw the ourang-
outang pick up the stone and pound the earth.

Four Characters simultaneously, or overlapping:

[8.] *Free will is to mind* what *chance is to matter.*
These views would make a man a predestinarian of
a new kind, because he would tend to be an atheist.

[9.] It may be doubted whether a man can
intentionally wag his finger from mere caprice.
*It is chance which way it will be,
but yet it is settled by reason.*

[10.] We may fancy there is free will,
as we fancy there is such a thing as chance. *Chance
governs the descent of a farthing, free will determines our
throwing it up.* Equally true the two statements.
I verily believe free will and chance are synonymous.

[11.] Thinking over these things one doubts existence of freewill. *Shake ten thousand grains of sand together and one will be uppermost. So, in thoughts, one will rise according to laws.* Every action determined by hereditary constitution, example of others, or teaching of others.

Three Characters simultaneously, or overlapping:

[12.] Changes *not* result of *will* of animal, but *law of adaptation*, as much as acid and alkali. There is nothing stranger in death of species than individuals.

[13.] The sensation of fear is accompanied by beating of heart, sweat, trembling of muscles. Are not these the effects of violent running away & must not this running away have been the usual effects of fear in *animals*.

[14.] Persecution of early astronomers. Chief good of individual scientific men is to push their science a few years in advance of their age. *If they believe and do not openly avow their belief* they do just as much to *retard* the cause of truth.

Two Characters simultaneously, or overlapping, but clearly audible and intelligible to the audience:

[15.] *Origin of man now proved. He who understands baboon would do more towards metaphysics than Locke.*

[16.] Plato says that our 'imaginary ideas' arise from the pre-existence of the soul. *For pre-existence read monkeys.*

As a hideous crescendo is reached: a scream on the tape of the slave tortured by thumbscrews.

Then very very quiet. Characters all exit, silently.
All sound effects silent except distant typing (of monkeys)

Darwin speaks, quietly and calmly:

> DARWIN
> My father says that after insanity is over, people
> often think no more about it than of a dream.
> Insanity is produced by moral causes.
> Ideally by fear. Remember Chile earthquakes.

Pause. Darwin tosses an imaginary coin, and looks at the result.

> DARWIN *(deadpan)*
> Heads *and* tails.
> *(pause)* Right, marry Emma, it is then —

Darwin exits determinedly, Stage Left.

Lights come up on the two desks…

The Editor is sauntering away from his desk,
as he speaks, in a very BBC documentary voice,
to the subdued background sound of many many typewriters:

> EDITOR
> … And so Darwin did indeed marry his cousin,
> Emma Wedgwood, at the end of January 1839.
> They had already secured the house in
> Gower Street, which was to be their home
> till the move to Down House in —

> WRITER *(interrupts)*
> Er, excuse me for asking.
> But why are you dictating?
> Have you somehow gotten voice recognition
> software on that typewriter?

EDITOR

What on earth are you talking about?
I have a secretary, of course. Can't have a typewriter
without a lady typist. Name of Julia.
Very modern woman. Her voice is far too soft and
low, of course, not author-itative enough,
to be a writer herself. But an excellent secretary.
Division of labour, you know. That's Progress.

*Editor glances casually behind him —but there is no sign of 'Julia.'
In shock, Editor sees that there is a long series of monkeys pounding
away at typewriters, stretching behind him, to infinity —
either projected and animated, if possible, or as a cardboard cut-out
cartoon, perhaps concertina-ed out from the back of the Editor's
bookcase, or forwards from the Beagle ship.*

EDITOR

Now *that* is definitely going too far.
I'm not sure I'm going to contribute
anything more to this farrago.

WRITER

I'm not sure either. Let me think about it.

EDITOR

You're still misleading your audience, you know.
Charles did manage to think his way through
to the main lines of his theory even before they
were married. But you really should not imply
that he had made up his mind in 1839.
He waited nearly twenty years before he published
— you should know that. So celebrating evolution
at this stage is pretty premature.

WRITER

If you say so. *(addresses audience directly:)*
So: can you come back in twenty years? *(Exeunt.)*

INTERVAL

ACT TWO

[SCENE SIX]

*When the audience return from the interval, the stage is dominated
by a huge Book which stands vertically towards the middle of the stage.
It is open, with a double-page spread, showing:*

*Left: a sober frontispiece photo of Charles Darwin, 1859
Right: the title page of On The Origin of Species, 1859*

*Enter into a spotlight at one side of stage, a traditional
ONE-MAN-BAND: harmonica,, leg cymbals, back and snare
drum, but also with a digitally enhanced keyboard / synthesiser
hanging from his neck.
The Band provides suitable musical interventions and FX throughout
this scene.*

Roll on drum to introduce:

*Enter into a travel spotlight at other side of stage:
COMPERE, dressed as a Master of Ceremonies from an old style
Music Hall, and 'barks' and enunciates accordingly:*

>COMPERE *(enthusiastically welcoming)*
>My Lawds, Lay-dees, and Gentel-ehmen,
>Paying *Touristes*, National Newspaper Crrrr-itics —
>and any Ape Ancestors or Grandmother Gorillas
>happily present here in the audience tonight —
>It is my profoundest pleasure and particularly
>peculiar privilege to perform the perennially popular
>practice of presenting, for your delirious delectation
>and in-describable de-light, the fabulous and
>fantastical findings of our very own world-
>renowned botanical boffin, Mr Charles Darwin, —
>whose astonishingly advantageous educative
>advances, and astoundingly adventurous
>endeavours, have recently brought to you,

and to the entire perusing and paying public of
these noble islands — not forgetting our ineluctably
and insatiably curious fellow-chimpanzees —
an almost unutterably unbelievable and
unparalleled account of the very existence of our
noblest of species. So, without any further pre-
posterously pre-tentious post-ponement,
with no more painfully pseudo-alliterative pre-
tences of pusillanimous or parsimoniuous pro-
crastination —we give you: the results of his
(crescendo, with Band accompaniment:)]
scientifico- / mathematico-/ logico-/ deductivo-/
demonstrative-/ empirical-/ experimental
Hypothesis: his book entitled On The Origin of
Species By Natural Selection, first edition,
hot off the press, guaranteed no misprints,
in this year of grace 1859.
(rousing fanfare from Band)
With a very special thank-you to all our monkey
friends for typing endlessly away back there.
They're doing the Complete Works of Wikipedia
Shapeskeare next.
Now, to get you all nicely warmed up after that long
interval of twenty years, will the gentlemen in the
audience please select the nearest young lady within
reach, —place their left hand experimentally upon
her right knee—and give a gentle squeeze.
(FX of 'Whoops' from all round the auditorium)
I thaaaank you. I see we have lots of gentlemen
in tonight. Warmed up nicely. And now my loverly
assistant, Ms Twankey, will display her
undoubtable delights for you —

Enter WIDOW TWANKEY, suitably attired.

She turns a page of the book, to reveal a new double-page
Left page: the famous 'ape' caricature of Darwin;
Right page : the words of the Song Chorus.

COMPERE *(as the book page turns).*
Is it open? Oh no it isn't! Oh yes it is!
Right, my gentle audience: Hymn 42!

Widow Twankey & Compere first sing the Chorus together,
while a bouncing yellow ball with a smiley face on it is projected onto
the Chorus words on the Book page. Audience encouraged to join in.

Then Widow Twankey & Compere sing the verses alternately,
with the audience singing the chorus repeats:).

Chorus:
Am I Satyr or Man?
Pray tell me who can,
And settle my place in the scale.
A man in ape's shape,
An anthropoid ape,
Or a monkey deprived of his tail?

TWANKEY
The "Vestiges" taught
That all came from nought,
By "development" so called "progressive"
That insects and worms
Assume higher forms
By modification excessive.

COMPERE
Then a medical lad
(With a rather fat dad)
Fancied himself as a sailor
And when he returned
From his trip round the world
He presented this tale to his tailor:

(rousing repeat of Chorus)

COMPERE
"Now listen old fruit
I've got to the root
Of the story of man's first creation
Old Adam and Eve we safely can leave —
A monkey was our first relation."

TWANKEY
Then Darwin set forth
In a book of much worth
The importance of "Natural Selection"
How the struggle for life
Is a laudable strife
And results in "specific distinction."

(repeat of Chorus)

TWANKEY & COMPERE *duet:*
So let pigeons and doves
Select their own loves
And grant them a million of ages.
Then doubtless you'll find
They've altered their kind
And changed into prophets and sages.

COMPERE
Now, Widow T'Wank, would you like to
'play a game with me', as the bishop said to
the actress: You be BishopWilberforce —
it's time we had women bishops! — and I'll be
Professor Huxley! *(Compere puts on false side-whiskers)*
And we can play: 'The Insult Game!'

*Compere turns another page of the Book to show large cartoons of
Wilberforce and Huxley.
As he does so, Twankey disappears behind the book and comes
back—quick change artiste— dressed in bishop's robes and a mitre.
Compere and Twankey both don huge boxing gloves and thump each
other at the end of each following exchange. Cymbals and drum rolls as:*

TWANKEY-WILBERFORCE
I would first like to ask Professor Huxley:
Is it on his grandfather's side or his grandmother's
side that he is descended from an ape?

FX from digital keyboard Band: synthesised cheers. Drum beat.

COMPERE /HUXLEY
A man has no reason to be ashamed
of having an ape for a grandfather.
(FX: synthesised boos)
If there were an ancestor whom
I should feel shame in recalling,
it would rather be a man,
endowed with great ability and a splendid position,
who should use these gifts to obscure the truth.

FX: synthesised boos. Clash of cymbals, roll on drums, boos and cheers

TWANKEY-WILBERFORCE
You, sir, believe in a succession of your ancestors
leading back to a hairy-tailed quadruped,
the uncouth inhabitant of woods and jungles.
Whereas I, sir, believe in the Apostolic Succession,
that noble line of Anglican Bishops
stretching back to the Saviour himself.

FX: artificial "OOOH"s

COMPERE-HUXLEY
May I assure my Lord Bishop that I have no
difficulty whatsoever believing in the Apostolic
Succession. *(pause)* How else could one explain
the continuity between my Lord Bishop of Oxford
—and Judas Iscariot.

FX: synthesised boos. Cymbals, drum roll etc.

TWANKEY-WILBERFORCE
Do you deny, sir, the miracles upon which
belief in christianity rests secure?

COMPERE-HUXLEY
I agree, my lord bishop, that the christan religion
was at first attended with miracles, and that even
at this day *(pause)* it cannot be believed in by any
reasonable person—without a miracle.

FX: synthesised cheers, boos, etc.

TWANKEY-WILBERFORCE
So, professor, after all your scientific observations
and rationalist inquiries, what has your study
of the creation told you of its glorious creator?

COMPERE-HUXLEY
That he has an inordinate fondness for beetles.

Music: brief snatch of Beatles: 'Can't buy me love'.

COMPERE
(tears off false side-whiskers and boxing gloves)
Oh widow twank,
I can't keep up this pretence any longer.

TWANKEY
Can't keep anything else up either, so I've heard.

COMPERE
Take those episcopal togs off. Be my Gal!

Twankey disrobes, to strip-tease music from Band,
modulating into sweet courtship music.

COMPERE
Oh, my twankey widow, your ears are like petals—

TWANKEY
— bicycle petals.

COMPERE
Your teeth are like stars —

TWANKEY
— they come out at night
(she smiles: several teeth missing)
Big gap in the fossil record there!

COMPERE
Your cheeks are like peaches —

TWANKEY
— all pink and hairy.

(Twankey puts on ape mask:)

COMPERE
Be my Love!

Compere and Twankey sing duet, to suitable music from Band.

DUET
Oooh. Doo bee doo bee doo
I wanna be like you
Wanna walk like you
Talk like you
You'll see it's true
A man like me
Can be an ape like you—

*Interrupted by Jemmy Button, in Panto Buttons uniform,
on unicycle, or hobby- horse, waving a telegram. FX Fanfare.*

JEMMY
Telegram! *(reads it out:)* From *The Producers:*
Enough! Desist this cacophonous celebration!
Adapt this show immediately!

Jemmy Button exits to FX Fanfare. The Book falls flat (forwards), revealing behind it the glittering gymnastic apparatus of the game show. The PRESENTER, in star-spangled suit and the usual smarm, makes a magnificent entrance. Fanfares.)

PRESENTER

I am Your Presenter-Producer, Fabulous Forsooth! To see you, nice. Loverly. Right, lads and lasses, we're fed up with all this antedeluvian entertainment. Pantomime. Music Hall. Rubbish! Got to adapt, change with the times, get up-to-date, with-it. What we need is a Game Show, contestants, audience participation, prizes, phone-ins, on-stage adverts, sports sponsorship. *(FX: synthesised Ooohs etc.)* So: are you ready for: "The Great (Big) Game Show: Get Fitted!!" (FX Fanfares as he gestures at the apparatus) Olympics training thrown in! Right, we need two audience volunteers. Let's see, anyone in the audience called: Cinderella? Snow White? Sleeping Beauty? Ugly Sister? Madonna? No?? Any fellah called Robin Hood, Ali Baba, Prince Charming, David Beckham? This isn't getting us anywhere. Have to use more modern methods. Random selection. A Lottery. *(takes out large mobile phone)* My Random Number Generator: rings the changes! Cod, Lizard, Parrot, Woman! *(he punches a number on each word—a phone apparently rings under specific seat in audience.)* Under your seat, love. Pick it up! —and Come on Down!

Compere goes into the audience to escort demure young Lady. As Lady makes her way to stage:)

PRESENTER

Right, who have we got? A young lady? Great tradition in the English theatre:

so long as she's got long legs, a girl can play
principal boy or un-principled lady.
Has she got long legs? Yes! OK, it's a delightful
little lady. Right, one woman, one man?
Have to take our chances here. When a woman
meets a woman. 50-50? 1 in 3 chance? Ever heard
of Mendelian Genetics. Great Band. Right:
Finch, Woodpecker, Bat, Man!
(rings number—phone rings in audience.)
Gotcha! Yes, A Man. You sir,
the one with the glasses. Behind you!,

While Widow Twankey goes into the audience to escort the Man:

PRESENTER
(to Lady, giving her no time to reply:) Now, what's your
name, dear? And where are you from? Lovely.
Willing to take part? Yes. And your prize, just for
taking part, my darling, a copy of the very rare
first edition, with the misprint. And if you win,
the key to the door of your very own two-up two-
Down House. So: Take your clothes off !!
(FX strip-tease music begins, Lady looks askance, protests)
Come on, don't be shy.
This is Family Entertainment.

*Compere whips off the Lady's dress, revealing a skimpy Classical
Maiden costume, fetchingly off-shoulder. He arranges her at one side of
the stage, chained to a broken classical column — so far hidden behind
the One Man Band.)*

PRESENTER
Ma Donna Mia!! *(by now the Man has reached the
stage—to Man:)* And She, sir, is *your* prize.
Oh You Lucky Lucky Man! So: get your kit off.
What you waiting for?

Man quickly takes off his jacket: has a Superman T-shirt underneath.

PRESENTER
Cheat.

Man strips futher: a Victorian Strong Man costume underneath:
leopard-skin tights and braces. Twankey hands him a large false
moustache. And some fake dumbells.

PRESENTER
But first, you have to *win* your prize.
Because she's worth it. So, you have to have
a *Competitor.* Are you ready to play : "The Survival of
the Fattest!" Against Darwin's very own
great-great-grandfather: Erasmus Kong!

A large cage is wheeled onstage by a Victorian Policeman from Punch
and Judy, ("Evening, all."), armed with a huge phallic sausage as his
weapon to control the large Gorilla which is inside the cage. The
Gorilla is in an obvious Gorilla costume, and wearing polka dot shorts;
he rattles cage bars, roars, etc.

PRESENTER
Enter The Beast ! And there's the Beauty,
My Fair Lady over there.

Gorilla thumps chest, howls, etc. Lady cowers melodramatically away.

PRESENTER
Right, let me explain the rules to you both:
What you have to do is: —

The Presenter gives a brief rapid outline of the genuinely tricky
gymnastics routine on the elaborate apparatus:
(e.g:) climb a ladder, swing across a gap, shinny down pole, etc.
Details depend on the designer for the game apparatus, but the patter
should include appropriate phrases such as: 'go up the scale of creatures'
[ladder], 'across the punctuated equilibrium' [tightrope], take one of
'nature's little leaps' [jump], slide down the 'descent with modifications'
[slide], etc. etc.

*Basically, the contest is to be started by both Man and Gorilla racing
up separate ladders, then fighting each other on a single tightrope,
to be the first down a chute—as elaborate as can look feasible.*

*Throughout the Presenter's spiel the clearly uncomprehending Gorilla
is regularly thumped on the head by the Policemen's sausage.
The Man flexes muscles, twirls dumbells, waxes moustache, does push
ups etc. The Lady simpers coweringly.*

PRESENTER
Right, let the Beast out of his cage. And: Begin!

Presenter fires starting pistol.

*The Gorilla is let out of the cage, but stands still,
dumbly gazing at the Lady. Doesn't even start the contest.*

*Meanwhile, very skilfully, the Man climbs ladders, swings from ropes,
etc etc.*

*Gorilla waits, scratching its head in apparent incomprehension,
until the Man has very nearly finished—*

*Then Gorilla grabs the starting pistol from Presenter Forsooth
and shoots the Man, who falls..*

*Gorilla grabs the Lady, puts her over his shoulder and runs
off stage with her. Fay Wray-type screams from the wings.*

PRESENTER
Gone back to hisown planet, I see.
Well, folks, not quite what we expected.
Does Brute Cunning win the day?. Surely no.
But: *(consults a little book)* it says in the rule book here
that: 'Dead people are disqualified'.
Not like Big Brother you know.
So, our friend Gorilla George has to be the winner.
And the race must go on. Big round of applause!
And get that body off the stage.

*Either: the game show apparatus, cage, one man band, etc are cleared off the stage rapidly, leaving the Presenter alone.
The Book is still lying flat. Or: see * below.*

PRESENTER
All good clean British Fun. But seriously, folks.
Some of you probably came here for an educational
play about Charles Darwin, and the management
will have to oblige you. We cater for all tastes here.
So: what we need now is: a nice bit of smut, smut,
smut. Sex. Scandal. Skeletons lurking in cupboards.
The Sun Says: Monkey Business in Darwin Closet.
These modern biographers must have dug up
some dirt on him. OK, got the script here:
(pulls script out of pocket) Next scene looks promising:
"Darwin and the New Woman : His passionate
encounter with his favourite niece, Julia
Wedgwood." Niece, nudge nudge.
An emancipated woman, it says here.
Know what I mean, nudge nudge. Better and
better. "A Dolls House episode. " Sorry, "Down
House" episode, 1869. "Photographic realism."
Henry Gibson. Whatever.
OK, let the good sets roll. Action!

Presenter exits.

*Preferably: the back of the flat Book now unfolds beautifully into a
Pop-Up box-set of Down House study, constructed from full-scale
black-and-white photos. Reminiscent of 'Goodnight Moon' pop-up
book, but ultra-realistic, with a useable door in rear of the set.*

*Or: flat Book has earlier been wheeled off stage at * above,
and the Platform now rolls out, with the Down House study in
meticulous realist mode, preferably again as a photographic set.*

*Stage-hands place a real table, with a plant and props, and two chairs
on the set.*

60 year-old Darwin takes his seat, preferably not the same actor as the Darwin of Act I.

[SCENE SEVEN]

Down House 1869. Late afternoon light.

Darwin aged 60, is sitting in his Down House study.
He is playing a bassoon, very badly, to a climbing plant nearby.
On a small table are freshly-served tea, scones, etc. jostling for space with books and a manuscript. Allow bassoon to continue briefly.

Enter, behind Darwin, Julia Wedgwood, aged 30-something. (in real life, deaf). She moves silently behind Darwin and puts her hands over his eyes. The bassoon emits a startled noise.

> DARWIN
> Ah, let me see. *(feels hands)* Too soft for Francis.
> And it doesn't feel like Henrietta—

> JULIA
> One more guess—

> DARWIN
> Julia. Of course. Julia
> *(She takes her hands away and comes round in front of him)*

> DARWIN
> My dearest Julia.
> What an exceedingly pleasant surprise.

> JULIA
> Uncle Charles. It *is* good to see you.
> *(She kisses him on both cheeks.)*

> DARWIN
> And with your usual exquisitely efficient sense of
> punctuality, you have arrived just in time for tea

JULIA *(laughs)*
I actually arrived ten minutes ago, but I told
Auntie Emma that I wanted to surprise you —
though she warned me that you rather dislike
surprises.

DARWIN
But this is a *delightful* surprise, dear child.
Now, be seated and help me to sample this
delicious superfluity of scones— while I see if
Emma has provided a second cup—She has indeed.
Careless— I might have tumbled your little game.

JULIA
But we knew you were far too engrossed in your
bassoon to bother yourself with tea for a while. Did
I interrupt your experiment at a crucial moment?

DARWIN
Well, I don't know what my startled wrong note
will do to it, but I'm confident the plant will survive.
It has exceedingly little aesthetic sense, as yet,
I'm afraid. *(hands her a cup of tea)*

JULIA
Are you really trying to teach it the finer points
of Mozart?

DARWIN
Certainly not with my playing! No, I'm simply
curious as to why plants move quite as they do,
why one climbs this way, another curls that way.
What really are they sensitive to? Light certainly,
heat too. But perhaps sound also.
Does music move them? *(Julia mock-groans)*
At any rate, it pleases me to exalt plants in the
overall organic scale—even if they do have to
endure my execrable scales in the process.
Do you know that plants sleep at night.
Hardly anyone believes they do.

JULIA
Ah, but do they dream?

DARWIN
Always the same Julia. Always the impossible
question. The true philosopher.

JULIA *(sips tea)*
Have you never taken an interest in philosophy?

DARWIN *(teasing)*
Once. Only once. Let me see, when was it?
Nearly ten years ago now. A quite fascinating article
by a brilliant young woman. *Macmillans Magazine.*
It was entitled, I believe, 'The Boundaries of
Science.' I was quite captivated by it.

JULIA
Now you're teasing me. And I have written
other articles since.

DARWIN
Yes, I know, Julia. But I'm afraid I have never
had a taste for these things. Are you still writing
your great philosophical work, and is it to astound
and illuminate us all?

JULIA
Slowly, Uncle Charles, very slowly.

DARWIN
The best way, Julia, the best way — but not the best
way to eat scones. Do help yourself — they too are
sensitive to heat: they go cold quickly. And you still
haven't told me why I am enjoying the immensely
pleasurable surprise of your visit.

JULIA
Well, partly because I missed your 60th birthday
celebrations. I had a quite wretched cold
and my doctor forbade me to travel.

DARWIN
Yes, Hensleigh told me you were unwell —
so I did not feel piqued at the absence of my
favourite neice. And I did receive your present —
though I confess that its pages are still ever so
slightly — uncut.
(he picks up a book lying amongst others)

JULIA *(teasing)*
But its pages don't need to be cut, Uncle.
You haven't even opened it.

DARWIN
Well, I did get as far as the title page.
I do read very very slowly, after all.
But I'm afraid, Julia, that at my age you will
never convert me to philosophy. *(opens book and reads
from the title-page:)* Mr Immanuel Kant,
The Critique of Pure Reason. The very title sent a
shiver through my empiricist soul.

JULIA *(laughs)*
Ah, but a pure empiricist couldn't know
he had a soul!

DARWIN
Oh, dear, sharp as ever Julia. I shall take your most
emphatic word for it—provided you take some
more tea—and provided you tell me why
you really came. My birthday was weeks ago.
What is the other pure reason?

JULIA *(hesitant)*
The difficult part. I need, I think, advice.
But not quite advice. I need to understand
something— I have received a proposal.

DARWIN
Indeed? Of marriage? Am I to congratulate you?

JULIA
Yes, you may congratulate me.

DARWIN *(pleased)*
In that case, indeed I do. Most warmly.
And am I allowed to know—

JULIA
—who has been so foolish.

DARWIN
Not at all! Who has been so fortunate—
if you are going to accept him.

JULIA
That's what I need your advice about,
Uncle Charles..

DARWIN *(puzzled)*
In that case, don't I rather need to know who it is...

JULIA
No, Uncle. I don't want your advice—or anyone's
—about marrying this man or that.
That's my decision, thank you.

DARWIN *(more puzzled)*
The independent Julia. As you wish.
But then, what advice—or understanding—
am I to be called upon to provide?

JULIA

That's what I find difficult. Even to formulate.
(she gets up restlessly, thinking, and prowling the room;
picks up manuscript from table:) Is this your current
book, Uncle Charles?

DARWIN

Yes. *The Descent of Man.* Murray has just offered me
a contract, so I am pushing ahead with it
as well as I can. —But that wasn't what you came
to talk about, Julia. Is it about *your* book?

JULIA

In a way, it is—

DARWIN

Come, sit down, tell me.

JULIA

(continues to pace; then turns to face him:)
Aunt Emma told me years ago that you had already
arrived at your theory of Natural Selection even
before you were married. Yet you didn't publish it
till over twenty years later. That's what I think
I want to understand.

DARWIN *(very puzzled)*

I don't see the connection, Julia.

JULIA

(pauses, then sits facing him directly; decisively, quickly:)
For eight years now I've been working on my book.
But it's gradually changed into a different book.
Yet the same. I wanted to investigate the limits of
purely rational inquiry, to draw a clear line between
ordinary understanding and scientific reasoning
on one side, and religious belief and faith on the
other. Do you understand?

DARWIN
Remember, I'm not a philosopher, Julia.
Though I did read John Locke once. *An Essay Upon
Human Understanding.* *(joke:)* I didn't understand it.

JULIA *(laughs)*
Perhaps I should use you as an example of the
limits of understanding. *(serious:)* I began by working
on John Stuart Mill's *Logic.* I wanted to define
the limits of logic, the areas where argument
and reasoning could not go, where logic was
inappropriate. But then I kept on being told that
since women can't think logically in the first place,
I was the last person to investigate the limits of
logic. That angered me.

DARWIN
Well, your anger was a perfectly logical reaction,
at any rate.

JULIA
Thank you, Uncle Charles. But I still needed to
answer the objection, rationally. And how could I
—or anyone—prove that my thinking about the
limits of logic was itself—logical? I was trapped,
locked inside my own problem. But then I realised
that there was another *kind* of approach: to try to
see *why* people think that women are illogical.

DARWIN
I'm afraid I'm getting lost in all this logic, Julia.
I still don't see the connection.

JULIA
I don't *see* it either—but I do know it, I *feel* it.
That's what I'm now working on: a critique of logic,
a critique of liberty, an inquiry into the subjection of
women. Somehow it *is* the same issue. And Mill
himself has moved in the same direction—*(sudden
apparent switch:)* When you married Aunt Emma,

did you know that your ideas on evolution,
on religion, would deeply shock her,
would pain and hurt her?

DARWIN
Ah, I see. No, Julia, there was an element of that,
certainly—but it wasn't why I delayed for so long.
You fear that your own ideas would pain and hurt
the man you wish to marry? Is that it?

JULIA *(puzzled herself)*
Yes, that is part of it. But something more than that.
Something inside me tells me that marriage,
a family, would hold me back, delay my work
intolerably, perhaps make it impossible.
Not just the practical difficulties. Something
I can't grasp. But I feel I really can't do both.

DARWIN *(quite a long pause)*
I think you are wrong Julia. And I suspect that
your worries about marriage are really only an
excuse. Eight years. A long time. But not a long
time. I spent eight years just working on barnacles.
Three months dissecting a minute mollusc,
no bigger than a pinhead. Pure tedium.
But it was necessary. It always is. And that is what
I suspect you are afraid of. Your book is obviously
ambitious, Julia—but you want to finish it quickly,
urgently. And you can't. All the rest is a roundabout
way of not facing that. It's much simpler than you
think, Julia. I had the theory, yes—as perhaps you
do, already. But even a page or two can take a year
to *prove*. Can seeds germinate after they have been
in sea-water for three months? Well, you have to
wait three months to find out.

JULIA
But not twenty three years! That's what puzzles me.
How could you delay that long? *That's* what
I'd like to understand.

DARWIN
Well, yes. I admit it wasn't only the facts.
The conclusions needed time too. Because some
conclusions are most unpalatable, Julia.
And perhaps, Julia, just perhaps, what you feel,
what you know, is the same problem:
that in the end your own conclusions will be
unpalatable, not just to others but to you.

JULIA
But I don't even know what kind of facts
I need to investigate. It's not as simple as your seeds
in sea-water, Uncle Charles. And I certainly don't
have any conclusions yet. That's my problem.

DARWIN
You always know what you want to prove,
at some level. But it may not be the conclusion
you actually arrive at. And you may not like it
even if you do. You already know, Julia, that you
will have to face the facts of natural history if you
want to prove that women can be the equal of men.
And that will be very difficult. The male of the
human species, like most animal species, has
certainly established himself as much the more
powerful of the two sexes. And unless there is some
quite elemental change in the whole human
environment, I at least would have to say—
simply as a naturalist—that it is most unlikely that
he can be made to relinquish that position.
Most unlikely. You know that too Julia.

JULIA
Men and women adapt to their environment, yes.
So the environment has to change, yes. But women
are *part of* the environment for men, as men are for
women. If women change *themselves*, isn't *that* an
elemental change in the whole human environment?

DARWIN
Yes. *If* you have the power to change yourselves.
But what real power do you have against men
who don't want you to change?

JULIA
At least I have the power to say
No to this proposal.

DARWIN
Perhaps you do, but a concerted No from all
women would be suicide for the species,
would it not?

JULIA
We don't just have the power to say No.
But to choose our partners.

DARWIN
Do you—? Really? Freely?

JULIA
Of course we do. At least now.

DARWIN
Well, yes, I agree that forced marriages are rather
out of fashion, this century at least. *(smiles)*
But I meant more than that. A real *choice*.
Beyond reason. Beyond necessity. Is that really
possible? Natural Selection has little place
for that kind of free choice. Its selection is based
not on freedom but on the necessity to survive,
as a species, to propagate the next generation.
Certainly I used to think that free will and natural
necessity were, in the end, the same. *(pause)*
You want to know why I delayed for so long in
publishing my theory. Perhaps I can show you why.
It might help. *(gestures)* In that small oblong box
on the table. Would you open it for me please.

JULIA *(opens box)*
Feathers?!

DARWIN
Yes, a handful of feathers. I always keep just a
handful near me. To remind me of what is
most difficult - and most unpalatable. *(he takes some
feathers out of the box and holds them cupped in his hand
while he speaks:)* People objected to my theory
because they didn't want to share a common
ancestor with the ourang-outang at the zoo.
But I knew that was true. So I accepted it.
That wasn't difficult. But then: one day, I was
cutting open a Galapagos finch. I was intrigued
by how their beaks had adapted to different feeding
environments and wanted to see if there had been
any corresponding adaptations in their digestive
systems. But their plumage was of no real
significance and generally very dull. So I simply
collected the feathers up and was about to throw
them away when I absent-mindedly let them trickle
through my fingers—like this:

*He raises his hand and lets the feathers fall slowly to the floor.
They both watch until all the feathers settle.)*

*The long speech that follows should be a quiet speech,
not argumentative, but meditative, and almost to himself.*

DARWIN
A simple gesture. Feathers falling.
But Newton is supposed to have discovered the
theory of gravitation from watching an apple fall.
Perhaps so. And Newton's physics will, in principle,
explain why each of those feathers falls precisely
the way it does and lands precisely where it lands.
Gravity and the movement of the air. But could we
ever know enough to say why *that* feather fell *there*
and not *there (points to one).* We would have to chart
every breath of air upon the globe.

An impossible task. Yet possible, in principle.
(pause)
Already, on the Beagle, Captain Fitzroy
was trying to establish a science of the weather.
He wanted to chart not just the sea but every breath
of wind, every cloud. And he was right.
In principle, we can do so. But I do not wonder
that in the end he lost his reason— and then took
his own life.
(pause)
And I was engaged in an equally impossible task.
I was trying to explain how thousands of species
had developed in precisely the way they had.
Why that feather was blue not white.
Eight years on barnacles. But every scientist knows
that we can never explain *all* the details.
We can only suggest the guiding principles,
the broad explanatory laws.
(pause)
But then—looking at those feathers on the floor
around me—the *real* difficulty finally struck me.
When, as scientists, we propose those general laws,
we imply that there is a *pattern*. Though we cannot
see it, those feathers do form an *intelligible grouping*.
Each falls precisely where it does partly because
the others fall precisely where they do.
They form a system. And so do species.
(pause)
But though there is a *pattern*, there is no *design*.
Just as there is *no design* in the fall of those feathers,
or in the shape of a cloud. That is what is the
most difficult, Julia. Difficult to grasp.
Difficult to accept. People want there to be a
design, not just a pattern, a purpose not just an
intelligibility. They see a pattern in the processes
of natural selection, and they want to call it
'progress'. They want an overall direction.
But there isn't one. Just many, many local
directions, overlapping particular patterns.

A struggle not a plan. A system, but not a design.
(longish pause)

And I, too, Julia, wanted there to be some *purpose*.
I wanted, most of all, to believe that suffering made
sense, led somewhere. But it doesn't. *(pause)*
Malthus taught me that most members of a species
have to die for some to survive and to propagate.
There is only enough room, enough food,
for far fewer than will naturally breed.
When it's a matter of insects, I can accept that.
But Malthus was talking about human beings.
And so, in the end, was I.
(pause)
Ten days after we moved into this house,
my little Annie died. And then Charles.
And now Susan, Caroline, even the beautiful
Charlotte, have all gone.
(pause)
Seeing those deaths as part of a pattern doesn't help
if the pattern itself has no more meaning than
those feathers on the carpet.
(pause)
And I wanted to believe that slavery would be
abolished, *had* to be abolished. Yet I found myself
writing about slave-bees, with their marvellously
mathematical architecture, the honeycomb,
and their complete social organisation—of total
slavery. On my own theory, were human beings
so very different after all? Five years ago,
the Southern slave-owners were still fighting
to be like those bees. It seems that our puny species
can make so very little difference even to the rest of
our own species—still less to the vast age-old forces
of nature, the global pattern of winds, tides,
weather, climate.
(pause)
And even my own life. That seemed to form a
pattern. Those five years on the Beagle
gave me enough work to last a lifetime.

But the pattern of my life rested on pure *chance* —
on your grandfather arriving home just at the right
time—And even then Fitzroy only accepted me on
board because he believed that he could tell a man's
character from the shape of his nose — and mine
just happened to be the right shape!
Without that, my voyage, my discoveries, my theory
wouldn't ever have happened.

He is about to go on, but Julia interrupts in gentle exasperation.

JULIA
All you're saying, Uncle Charles, is that if
Helen's nose had been a fraction longer
there would have been no Trojan war...

DARWIN *(laughs)*
And therefore no *Iliad* and no *Odyssey.*
Good Lord, a world without either the *Odyssey*
or the *Origin of Species*— and all because of noses.
Yes, I know, it's an old, old thought. A leaf in the
wind can change the destiny of a nation.
But men have always wanted to read their destinies,
even in the fall of a feather, the flight of a flock of
birds. Because men want to believe that something
else—*someone* else—makes sense of, guarantees,
their lives, their suffering, their struggle.
But there is no design. Only the constant struggle
of each generation to exist, to survive, to propagate
the next generation. *(pause)*
And each generation has to learn for itself that
there is no design, no guarantee, no purpose.
It wasn't the simple materialism of my theory
that I found difficult to accept. It was the sense
of sheer emptiness behind all that suffering.
I turned my mind away from that. For twenty years.
I still do.

JULIA

(pause, then quietly:)

And you think that our suffering, the struggle of
women for their own emancipation, is just another
local pattern, like the rest, entirely shaped by other
patterns, other struggles that we can't control.
Is that what you think that I'll find out for myself?
(pause)
But isn't *this* struggle different from all the rest?
If the most basic struggle is for the survival of the
species, for the propagation of the next generation,
doesn't that put women in a quite unique position,
at the crucial link in the chain? Our power to say
Yes or No determines who will breed the next
generation. Our choices may be apparently irrational
—like Fitzroy's choice of you because of your nose!
But we do make that kind of choice. Doesn't that
open up a gap in the chain, that moment of
yes *or* no: a space between nature and necessity.
Call it what you will: feminine caprice, romantic
irrationalism, love. But it's where pure materialism
breaks down. What Democritus and Leibnitz were
looking for: the swerve of the monad. Helen didn't
have to elope with Paris. Aunt Emma might not
have accepted you, Uncle Charles.

DARWIN

And Hensleigh might not have proposed to your
mother, but to someone else, Fanny perhaps.
The game of sexual selection, the old game.
A game of chance. But a competitive game too,
Julia. Paris made a *choice* as well, between three
women, three goddesses, in a competition.
Without that, the Trojan war would not have taken
place either. And it's in the element of competition
that the necessity resides in the end.

JULIA

You seem to *want* there to be necessity,
Uncle Charles — even though the thought of it
makes you sad. Why?

DARWIN

Perhaps necessity is simpler, Julia. For a scientist,
at any rate. Or perhaps I am simply getting too old
to believe again in freedom. It's a strange irony,
isn't it, that a man who has written so much on the
survival of the fittest should survive thirty years of
sickness—the nausea, vomiting, dizziness, the
headaches, insomnia and all the rest of it—
while Susan and Charlotte, and my dear Caroline,
all die before me. Yes, I am sad. I think all scientists
ought to die at sixty. They become too fixed in their
ideas. Their minds die. Like mine.

JULIA

Come, Uncle Charles. I'm sure you will write
ten more books while I slowly finish my first.
And if *you're* not here for your *70th* birthday
I at least shall most certainly be offended!

DARWIN *(laughs)*

Well, perhaps Julia. Yes, there is just one more book
I want to write. I started it thirty years ago.
Perhaps I shall finish it.

JULIA *(teasing)*
"The Critique of Pure Decision"?

DARWIN *(laughs)*

That would be your book, not mine.
My last book will be on worms. The common,
fascinating, garden earth-worm. In one year,
the worms on an acre of land bring to the surface of
the earth over eighteen tons of soil. Eighteen tons.
Those industrious worms. They put us all to shame.

JULIA

I think I can recognise a gentle hint, Uncle Charles.
You have your own work to do, and I have stayed
well past your tea-time.

DARWIN

As sharp as ever, Julia. Thank you.
Yes, my abominably large volume awaits.
It is time for more scribbling. *(pause)* But I feel
I haven't helped you at all. Will you write your
book, or get married? I think you could do both.

JULIA

You have helped. Perhaps I could do both.
But I now realise that it may be more important
to make the decision itself than either to write the
book, or to get married. Thank you. *(pause, half-
jokingly:)* But just in case I don't write my own book,
may I add just two words to yours?

DARWIN

The book on worms?

JULIA

No, 'The Descent of Man'. Should it not be
'The Descent of Man and Woman'?

DARWIN *(laughs)*

I shall think about that, Julia. But first,
I must finish my performance.
Ten minutes a day is the prescription,
and my poor plant still has three minutes to suffer.

JULIA

In that case I shall retire out of earshot immediately.
Write well, Uncle Charles.
(she goes over and kisses him)

DARWIN

Goodbye, Julia — and bless you.

Julia exits. Darwin picks up the bassoon and plays softly,
mournfully, briefly. Fade the lighting on the box-set.
Emma enters quietly and clears the tea-tray and bassoon,
then re-arranges the props for the next scene.
The Darwin actor may stay, or exit and return later
for the next Down House scene.

[SCENE EIGHT]

Lights fade up on stage, almost to house lights, but down on the Down
House platform-set.

Enter a man in casual dress, including jeans. He appears to be
smoking a dead cigarette. He wanders across the stage, preoccupied with
his own thoughts, but looking also at the set. Picks up a few feathers,
absent-mindedly. When he reaches centre down-stage he stops,
and suddenly looks directly at audience.

He speaks throughout to the audience, in a cross between a quiet
conversation and, switching suddenly, a maniacal stand-up comic
routine, combining Ross Noble with Jonathan Pryce in Trevor Griffiths
Comedians. Throughout, his face and features are extremely mobile.
Add a Max Wall physical energised use of the whole space of the stage
—except the Down House box-set.

He is preferably not the actor who played Writer in Act I.

He speaks all the following with constant and rapid shifts of voice, tone,
pace, accent, etc.

WRITER 2

—I've been thinking. Well, you could see that,
couldn't you. The slow, hesitant walk. The frowning
expression. The preoccupied fag. That *looks* like
thinking, doesn't it. It doesn't? Well, that's my
acting. I'm not really an actor, you see. I'm A
Writer. Yes, I know. The old trick. Where's
Pirandello when you need him, then?

—Why a writer? Well, I'm suicide prone, for a start. Endangered species. Species dying, with a dying pratfall. Come from a long line my gullible mother listened to. Apostolic Succession of con-men, liars, fraudsters, politicians, car-salesmen, on one side. And manic depressives, miserable sods, and advertising executives on the other. So I *had* to be a writer. No choice. In the genes, you see. *(gestures to jeans)* All I can afford.

—Species? Quote: "A species is a group of inter-breeding individuals who cannot breed successfully outside the group, so exclusive courtship rituals establish inter-breeding compatibility—otherwise a f***ing waste of time." Like mules. Writer!? Inter-beeding!? Huh! Can't even get a girlfriend. Where's my typist, home at tea-time? Take a French letter, Julia. You know I'm worth it. Still, I suppose death is a pretty exclusive courtship barrier. Death of the Author. ... Not yet, chummie.

— *(looks at set)* And this is Down House, is it? A museum. Must take a few photos. File them away. Call it research. Get a grant. *(looks again at set).* Of course, it's not. A Set. Design. Designer sets a speciality. Got an award for Scunthorpe.

—No, I was thinking. About science. Science is a funny thing, you know. Not funny, mind. You're not here for a comedy - are you? *(looks at dead cigarette)* You don't mind if I smoke? You're not allowed to, I'm sorry. Please extinguish all smoking individuals. Nosmo King. Despite what old Brecht howled: Let people smoke in my theatre—because he wanted people to *think* in the theatre. Well, I'm thinking. In the theatre. Well, smoking anyway.

—Actually, I'm not. Fire regulations. Theatre fires, dangerous business. Safety curtains. Have to be tested. OK, everybody leave. This is a safety drill.

Come back in twenty years. No, no. Please stay.
Please, I beg of you!

— I've been thinking. No, I've said that. Oh, yes:
I've been Thinking about Darwin. A play about
Darwin, that's what I've been thinking. Yup, I am
an actor, pretending to be *The Author*. Most of us
actors do that, don't we darlings. We just don't *need*
an writer, do we, dears. Can easily improvise a ten-
part epic, or two, The History Plays, workshopped
by Bill Shakes & Company. Before lunch.

— *(very manic:)* Inter-breeding. Coupling. Rub two
Boy Scouts together. Need two to make anything.
(Are there children present?) Father Dick
Christmas and Mother Twankey, shall we say.
Writer and Set. Game, set, and match-making.
Love All. Hardly. Have to be selective. Eleven-plus
would do nicely, thank you. Or just one *cornetto*. *Un*
homme et *une* femme. It's a reasonable percentage.
Or: a Producer and a Director. The Writer and The
Actress. The Bishop and The Actor. Darwin *and* the
Thee'ataar. Now, *there's* a pair of combinations for
you: The Evolution of the Theàt-er—In two semi-
random Acts. The pathetic struggle of the pit and
the pendulum of fashion.

— Where does it all start? Soliloquy? A sermon?.
A Pardoner's Tale. Or a lecture: they still call it a
lecture theatre. Or an operating theatre. Painful
business, the theatre. Or just a man in a pub,
telling a tall tale of Viking exploits and, er, erotic
escapades. Or some poor Fool, trying to jest the
night away for a debauched King or two. Then: add
another Voice, and you have: — a Ventriloquist!
Sorry, a Play. A two-hander. Very handy, small
budget. That's the thing. Add a third actor, of
course, step up to the platform, and you have the
classic formula for: —a bitchy argument.

—*(very fast:)* About Darwin. Make it DRAMATIC! Yelled the Producer. (Nobody expects the Producers! Respect, respect!) We're in a cut-throat business here. The pay's the thing. Survival of the fattest. Bums on seats. OK, Act I: Five years adventure, excitement. Round the globe. Revolutions, earthquakes, cut-throat Latin American bandits. The lot. *Very* dramatic. *If* you can put a damned earthquake on the stage. Or even a revolution. Or even a ship. For *five years*. Re-drawing nautical charts and collecting botanical specimens. Most exciting. Anybody for Galapogos Turtle soup?

— And then.*(slow down drastically)* Act II: Forty years. FORTY years. Forty years: a recluse, a sodding hypochondriac, living here, in Down House, never going anywhere, never seeing anyone, writing letters, doing 'SCIENCE' — oh, and taking long slow walks down the gravel path, — and being very ill, always. How in the name of the good ship Evolution do you *dramatise that?* Can we have a bit of gravel walk please? *(does slow walk across stage, to FX of crunching gravel)*. Thank you sound-man, every little helps. Waiting for Darwin. *[(rief FX of rain)* It's raining. What's the meaning of that, Check-hov? Global wetting?

— Darwin. Had the same problem. No, really, I mean it. He wasn't writing a play, of course. But the same *kind* of problem. Lots of data. All that data. And no shape. All those specimens. All those biographies. The letters. Fifteen volumes. So far. Man of Letters.

— And get the HISTORY RIGHT! Howled my Producer. No howlers, matey. So, can I have a research assistant, please, female, 18, long legs, or thereabouts. Fat chance. What 'History'? Born 1809. So was Tennyson. Great. Beethoven composed the *Emperor Concerto*. So? Exact same birth-day as Abraham Lincoln. What am I supposed to do with that? 1859. *Origin of Species.* And first oil-well drilled. First internal combustion engine. Busch invents the strip cartoon. So I'm supposed to throw in the Gulf War as well, am I? Sorry, wrong Busch: Wilhelm. Misprint. Dickens wrote *A Tale of Two Cities.* Ah, now there's that idea again. A breeding germ, a tricksy little sperm, worming its way into the fertile egg of my mushy brain—

— *Two* ideas! Rub them together. Seems a reasonable percentage. Cross-pollination. Original paper on natural selection, 1858: "A Joint Production by Alfred Wallace and Gromitt Darwin" no plagiarism, no priority issue. "Only sexual selection, the coupling of two of a kind, gives enough chance variation, genotype and phenotype, for possible evolutionary change." So: The Odd Couple: Darwin and *The Survival of the Genres.* Where's my lady typist?

— How do you give variation a *shape*? A piece of chance. A pattern on the carpet. Feathers. How do you dramatise a damn theory? Bertie Brecht had the same problem, of course. But at least Galileo got *condemned.* Darwin just got *headaches.* Ah, 1859: first industrial manufacture of aspirins! Gotcha!

—It's hopeless. You find yourself writing lines like: "Dr.Grant taught me everything I know about seaweed." Seaweed, I ask you: But it's *true.* A historical fact. Just so? So put it in. Like the feathers. Well, not really. I made that bit up. Most of the dialogue too. In fact, *all* of the damn dialogue. Never trust a Writer. Well, you have to, don't you. Make it up, I mean. Gap in the fossil record. Well, if you wanted to know the *truth* about Darwin, why didn't you go to the goddamn website. Julia should have had it up and running by now. So why am I here? *(looks at watch)*

—Actually, to be honest, I'm supposed to pick up those damn feathers. Can't leave them around for the next scene, he said. Destroy the illusion. "How do you get the feathers off the stage?" Shakespeare's problem. Well, I can't be bothered. There's only two scenes to go. Short ones. They can stay there till the end. Remind you. Stuffing geese, shooting pheasants, partridges, finches, whatever. White feathers in the snow. A pattern. Maybe.

—*(looks at watch again)* Right. Darwin should have aged enough by now. Forward ten years. Or back a hundred or so. Down House, 1880s—or thereabouts. Back to the facts, the letters, the books. Ready? Then let me get off.

— *(Starts to go, stops, turns—next passage in a perfectly serious informative voice:)*
The book Charles Darwin published between *The Descent of Man, or Sexual Selection* — as he finally called it — Julia might have approved—and his final book, on earth-worms, was entitled: *"The Expression of Emotions in Man and Animals."* A study of how chimpanzees and human babies learn and express emotions in the same way. The book includes an interesting discussion on *how actors express emotions on the stage.*

— *(back in manic role)* Stanislavsky learned a lot from that chapter. I think. Therefore: I am not —an Act--or. And we had to sack the other one. RSC trainee. Not up to it

— Right, now, a short fragment from the Moscow Arts Theatre. The sad, melancholy mode. Domesticated realism. A dying genre. Like 'em all. How does a genre survive? Support your Local Genre Preservation Society! Or: Watch it all come

down. The House of Bingo. After Miss Julia, the
Cherry Orchard, or Down Monkey House.
Or the other way round. 'Byee.

*Snaps his fingers and the lights come up on the box-set, but down on
the rest of the stage. Exits.)*

[SCENE NINE]

Down House. 1880s. Evening. The lamps are lit.
Darwin and Emma are seated at a table, playing backgammon.
*Francis Darwin, adult son, is seated in a chair; he is opening and
sorting the day's correspondence, including two small parcels
(containing a book and a pamphlet).*
*(Francis should preferably be played by the same actor as the Editor in
Act I. but this role can be adapted for: Henrietta, adult daughter.)*

Silence as the game continues between Darwin and Emma,
until Darwin loses a piece.

> DARWIN
> Luck! Pure chance, Emma.
> You can take no credit for that move.

> EMMA
> But you will still have to include it in my score
> if I win, Charles.

> DARWIN
> It should be against the rules. A move like that.
> Incredible! Well, I shall concentrate more.
> You shan't win the whole game, I assure you.

*Darwin concentrates with mock-ferocious attention. Francis gets up and
leaves the room.*
Pause

> DARWIN *(wins a piece)*
> There! Now that wasn't luck. I'm in form again.
> I feel myself about to win.

EMMA
But you still have to do so, dear.

DARWIN
I will, I will.

(more concentration.)

DARWIN
(pondering a move) Difficult. Difficult.
Yes, I see it. *(wins a piece)*

*Francis returns, carrying a book; sits again, and takes a letter
from the inside end-leaf of the book;and compares this letter with one
just received.*

Darwin finally wins the game.

DARWIN
Won! A Triumph! Another triumph.
(Darwin consults a small notebook on the table near him.)
That makes 2,490 games to you, Emma.
While I have now won a grand total of 2,795.

EMMA
But think of all the practice you have had with
Elizabeth. You have an unfair advantage there,
Charles.

DARWIN
Nonsense, my dear Emma, nonsense.
You are simply trying to excuse yourself
for losing *both* games this evening.

EMMA
As you wish, dear. Now, go and do your work with
Francis, while I put the board away. *(she does so)*

DARWIN
Well, Francis, how much is there this evening?

FRANCIS
Not a great deal, father. You wanted to thank
Huxley for his book and you said you had to write
to Romanes. There are some questions from the
reverend Ridley concerning Dr. Pusey's sermon;
yet another letter about vivisection; and two others,
one nominating you to the Berlin Academy and
one asking permission to dedicate a book to you.

DARWIN
Good, good. Let's begin with Huxley. Only a brief
note. Then Ridley and vivisection. Then the other
two. We can leave Romanes till last. Are you ready?

*Francis takes down Darwin's rapid efficient dictation in rapid efficient
shorthand : / indicates a brief pause in the dictation.*

DARWIN
(leafing through the volume from Huxley) To Huxley.
My dear Huxley. Very many thanks for sending me
your Science and Culture volume, / and I am sure I
will read most of the essays with much interest. /
However, / I wish that you could review your own
volume / in your old trenchant, combative style /
and then you could answer yourself / with equal
incisiveness / and thus, by Jove, you might go on *ad
infinitum*, to the joy and instruction of the world. /
Ever yours, very sincerely. etc.

EMMA
You do tease the man so.
I am surprised you are still friends.

DARWIN
Huxley will enjoy the joke. He once told me

that he wished that evolution had given him two heads—so that he could always have someone to argue with.

FRANCIS
Ridley next, I think. He specifies three questions which I've underlined.

(Francis hands a marked letter to Darwin, who reads rapidly through it, thinks for a moment, then dictates:)

DARWIN
Dear Sir, I have only skimmed through Dr Pusey's sermon, as published in the *Guardian*, / but it did not seem to me worthy of any attention. / As I have never answered criticisms excepting those made by scientific men, / I am not willing that this letter should be published. / But I have no objection to your saying that / Dr Pusey was mistaken in imagining that I wrote the *Origin* with any relation whatever to theology. / This answer disposes of your other two questions. / But I may add that, many years ago / when I was collecting facts for the *Origin* / my belief in what is called a personal God / was as firm as that of Dr Pusey himself. I remain, dear sir, yours faithfully, etc.

EMMA *(quietly)*
May I see Dr Ridley's letter, dear?

DARWIN *(hands it to her)*
Certainly, my dear. Let me know if you think I should add anything.

FRANCIS
Now vivisection, father. From Professor Lankester. He is simply canvassing opinions again and wants a brief response. I have copies of your letters to *The Times*. We could simply forward those to him.

DARWIN
Excellent, Francis, would you do that, please.
Emma, are you happy with the reply to Ridley?

EMMA
Of course, dear. Though it was perhaps a shade
abrupt. Mr Ridley is a sincere man, as indeed is
Dr. Pusey.

DARWIN
You're right, Emma. When you've written it up,
Francis, would you let me look over it again —
I can never decipher your shorthand —and I'll see
what might be added.

FRANCIS
Of course, father. The next one might please you.
From Professor Raymond du Bois. He has
proposed you for election as a Corresponding
Member of the Berlin Academy of Sciences.

DARWIN
(humorous, but genuine surprise) But I am *already* a
Corresponding Member of the Berlin Academy,
am I not, Emma? About a year ago, with Professor
Gray.

EMMA
That was surely the *French* Academy, Charles.

DARWIN
(even more surprised) Was it?

FRANCIS
Mother's right, father. It was the
Botanical Section of the French Institute.

DARWIN
Good Lord?. Well, in that case, we had better thank
Professor — *(he has forgotten the name)*

FRANCIS
Raymond du Bois.

DARWIN
Yes. To Professor.../ Thank you sincerely for
your most kind letter, / in which you announce the
great honour conferred on me... / er, with my
warmest thanks, yours most sincerely, etc.

FRANCIS
The next one is a request for permission to dedicate
a book to you. The handwriting is appalling.
Even worse than yours, father. But I *think* it's
from a Doctor Marx. A German, anyway.

DARWIN
The botanist?

FRANCIS
No, father. He says that he sent the first volume
of his work to you some time ago and now wishes
to dedicate the second volume to you. I checked
in your library, and found what seems to be
the volume. It is a work on political economy.

DARWIN *(startled)*
On what?!

*(Francis hands him the book he brought in earlier and
Darwin reads the title page:)*

DARWIN
"*Kapital: a Critique of Political Economy*" Yes, he *must*
be a German. These endless *Critiques*. Did we
correspond when he sent his first volume?

FRANCIS
Only one letter, father. A copy was inside the book
— just the usual letter: *(reads rapidly, carelessly:)*

"Dear Sir, I thank you for the honour which you have done me by sending me your great work on Capital; and I heartily wish that I was more worthy to receive it, by understanding more of the deep and important subject of political economy. Though our studies have been so different, I believe that we both earnestly desire the extension of knowledge, and that this in the long run is sure to add to the happiness of mankind. I remain, dear sir, yours faithfully, C. Darwin." That's all. But you may recall meeting a Mr Aveling—the delegation from the International League of Freethinkers. He is apparently the son-in-law of this Mr Marx. They are both freethinkers, and socialists, I believe.

DARWIN
Oh dear, these Germans. Why do they all have this foolish idea that there is some connection between socialism and evolution through natural selection. It's very tiresome.

EMMA
It's not only the Germans, Charles. The French tried to blame the Paris Commune on your theories.

DARWIN
Yes, I know. Just because the *Descent of Man* was published in the same year. And the Russian Czar banned the *Origin of Species* because he said someone had read it and tried to assassinate him. Well, one cannot be held responsible for *all* one's readers.

EMMA
I think you should definitely decline this dedication, Charles. It can do you no good to be associated with such people.

DARWIN
You're quite right, dear. I think a tactful but firm letter, Francis. Are you ready? *(dictates)*

"Dear Sir, I am much obliged for your kind letter. /The publication in any form of your remarks on my writings / really requires no consent on my part. / But I should prefer your volume *not* to be dedicated to me, / though I thank you for the intended honour, as this / — er — implies to a certain extent approval of the general publication, / about which I know nothing *(breaks off to pick up the volume of Kapital:)* Yes, that's true. I haven't even cut the pages. Sorry, Francis, no, don't include that. / I remain, dear sir, yours faithfully, etc." Is that the last of today's letters?

FRANCIS
Yes, that was the last.

Emma gets up and leaves the room.

DARWIN

Good, now we can concentrate on something far more important. A letter to Romanes if you please, Francis. *(dictates with more interest and energy:)* My dear Romanes, My manuscript on worms has finally been sent to the printer, / so I am going to amuse myself by scribbling to you on a few points. / New paragraph. / Your letter on intelligence was very — underline very — useful to me. / I have not attempted to define intelligence; but have quoted your remarks on experience, / and have shown how far they apply to worms. / It seems to me that they must be said to work with some intelligence. / Anyhow, they are not guided by a blind instinct. /New paragraph/ I do not know whether you will discuss in your book on the mind of animals, the intriguing case of the sand wasps, which *paralyse* their prey. / I suppose that the sand wasps originally merely killed their prey by stinging them in *many* places on the softest side of the body / and that to sting a *certain* segment was found by far the

most successful method. / And was inherited like
the tendency of a bulldog to pin the nose of a bull,
or of a ferret to bite the cerebellum. / It would not
be a very great step in advance to prick the ganglion
of its prey only slightly, / and thus to give its larvae
fresh meat instead of old dried meat./ My dear
Romanes, yours very sincerely, Charles Darwin.

*Emma has returned, carrying a book, in time to hear the last sentence
or so — and grimaces.*

DARWIN
Now we are truly finished for the evening.
Would you write those up for me please, Francis.
We really must get you a typewriter some day,
Francis.

FRANCIS
They'll be ready tomorrow father.
I hope mother has a good new novel for you.

DARWIN
Yes — one with a pretty heroine
and a delightfully happy ending? Have you Emma?

EMMA
I hope so. It's a new work by Mr Thomas Hardy.
You enjoyed his *Under the Greenwood Tree*,
I remember.

DARWIN
Yes, indeed I did. And what is his new work called?

EMMA
The Return of the Native.

FRANCIS
I shall leave you to enjoy it.
Good night, father. Good night mother.

DARWIN & EMMA
Good night Francis

Francis exits. Darwin settles himself in his chair and Emma begins to read the opening chapter of Return of the Native.)

EMMA
"Book First. The Three Women. Chapter One: A Face on which Time makes but Little Impression. A Saturday afternoon in November was approaching the time of twilight, and the vast tract of unenclosed wild known as Egdon Heath embrowned itself moment by moment. Overhead the hollow stretch of whitish cloud shutting out the sky was as a tent which had the whole heath for its floor.
Looking upwards, a furze-cutter would have been inclined to continue work; looking down, he would have decided to finish his faggot and go home. The distant rims of the world and of the firmament seemed to be a division in time no less than a division in matter.

*As Emma reads, the lights slowly fade. If possible, the entire set or platform recedes to the rear and out of sight. Emma's voice continues to be heard until bell tolls at ** below:*

EMMA
"The place became full of a watchful intentness now; for when other things sank brooding to sleep the heath appeared slowly to awake and listen. Every night its Titanic form seemed to await something; but it had waited thus, unmoved, during so many centuries, through the crises of so many things, that it could only be imagined to await one last crisis—the final overthrow—"

Lights on the Down House set fade out completely.

As the set / Platform recedes off-stage or into dark,
three Tombs appear from traps, slowly, majestically.
Or are disclosed by lighting-change.
If possible, completely bare stage except the tombs.
Single spot on each.
The tombs are upright, preferably with only faces visible in spots.
(as in Beckett's Play)
Perhaps an echo of the photo of Paris Communards in their coffins.

In the tombs: Tennyson, Darwin, Newton, all dead.

(If necessary, the Darwin actor rises from his chair as the reading
continues, and simply takes his place in the centre tomb.
But, preferably, the dead Darwin is played by the Darwin of Act I
and is in the tomb as it appears.)

As Emma's reading of the opening of Return of the Native finishes,
with "a final overthrow", a great bell tolls three times **.

Then Tennyson speaks in a resonant voice from his tomb:

[SCENE TEN]

    TENNYSON
    (reciting rather lugubriously—
    he is also composing as he recites:)
    And the suns of the limitless universe sparkled
    and shone in the sky
    Flashing with fires as of God, but we knew
    that their light was a lie —
    Bright as with deathless hope —
    but, however they sparkled and shone,
    The dark little worlds running round them
    were little worlds of woe like our own —
    No soul in the heaven above,
    no soul on the earth below,
    A fiery scroll written over with lamentation
    and woe, er, lamentation and woe

He is stuck and can't think of the next line, begins loud moaning,
trying to find rhyme:

> — and *woe,* — *so,* — *sorrow,* ....oh, no,—
> *(from now on, occasional moans of creative agony from*
> *Tennyon)*

NEWTON
Poor old Tennyson. I'm not sure that
he likes it here. Used to complain of
the cold flagstones when he first arrived.
Now all he does is moan that he's never seen Him.
I suppose he must be beginning to doubt
His existence. Have you ever seen Him, Darwin?

DARWIN
(who has had his eyes closed)
I do apologise, my dear Sir Isaac.
I was trying to ignore that racket —

TENNYSON
(moans very loudly)

DARWIN
— and didn't hear what you said.

NEWTON *(mishears)*
You were trying to ignore what I said—?'.

DARWIN
No. Tennyson's racket. What *did* you say?

NEWTON
I said, have you ever met Him?

DARWIN
Tennyson? Yes, once or twice.
Before death, that is. Not since, so far.
Only heard him, endlessly.

TENNYSON
(moans)

NEWTON
Not Tennyson. Him. It. Her. God.

DARWIN
Good Lord, no. How could I?
I'm not sure I even believe in Him. Her. It.

NEWTON
You don't have to believe in something
in order to see it, Darwin.
It's the other way round.

DARWIN
I'm sorry. I was never much of a philosopher.

NEWTON
Mind you, I'm not surprised you've never met Him.
I don't think He agreed very strongly with your
theories. He did have his own version, you know.

DARWIN
Yes, I suppose so. I do sympathise.
It's always difficult for the old to accept new ideas.
I feel it myself, after only a century or so.
I can't even understand all these new theories
they talk about when they come here these days.
What He must feel like, God only knows.

NEWTON *(drily)*
Precisely. *(pause)* You might have shown
a bit more respect, you know. I was always
very careful to leave a space for Him in my
calculations. I assume He was grateful.

DARWIN
I wouldn't be so sure, Newton.
Which would you rather be —
a mathematical anomaly in the ellipse of a planet,
or the descendant of a sea-urchin? Most people
I knew objected strongly enough to the latter.

NEWTON
I suppose you're right.

DARWIN
It's not easy being a scientist, is it?
Everybody blames you for taking the mystery
out of things — and then God disowns you as well.

NEWTON
Still, we do have Him to thank for this cathedral.

TENNYSON
(moans loudly)

DARWIN
Abbey, actually.

NEWTON *(mishears)*
Happy? Not really. Still, better than being a poet.
They really do suffer, don't they.

DARWIN
They pretend to. No self control. Invertebrates.

NEWTON
Invert-e-whats?

DARWIN
Technical term. No backbone. Primitive forms.

NEWTON

At least *I* left people with a nice shiny piece
of clockwork. What did *you* give them?
"Nature red in tooth and claw".

DARWIN

That was him, not me.

NEWTON

Come, come, you can't blame God
if you don't believe in him.

DARWIN

Not God. Tennyson.
It was his phrase, not mine.

NEWTON

Well, yours weren't much better.
The struggle for existence.
"The survival of the fittest."

DARWIN

That was Herbert Spencer's phrase.

NEWTON

Who?

DARWIN

Oh, just a 19th century English philosopher.

NEWTON

(sarcastically emphatic on each word:)
A *nineteenth century / English / philosopher?*
I don't believe *that*, at any rate.

DARWIN

We couldn't *all* be born in the 17th century.

NEWTON *(a palpable hit!)*
No, *that* would *really*
have put paid to your theory, wouldn't it.

TENNYSON
(moans very loudly, creative agonies still)

NEWTON
There he goes again. Dreadful, isn't it.

(They both listen. Tennyson stops. Pause.)

NEWTON
You have a great deal to answer for, Darwin.
Making people unhappy like that.

DARWIN
Me? I'm not responsible for Tennyson's moanings!

NEWTON
You are, in a way. You took away the purpose
in life. That made poetry *doubly* pointless.
You left people feeling that they were the result
of blind chance, a kind of endless grope to
nowhere. Whoever survived the struggle simply
showed themselves the fittest for another struggle.
Not much of a life, is it?

DARWIN
Well, it's not much of a death either.

NEWTON
You have a point. It doesn't add up to much, really.
But it's not too bad if you take it a bit at a time.
(TENNYSON moans) Or one moan at a time.
What a friend of mine called *moan—ad*s. *(pause)*
He's probably writing another verse.

DARWIN
I won't understand it if he does.
I couldn't read poetry even when I was alive.
Except Milton. I used to read a lot of Milton.

NEWTON
John Milton?

DARWIN
That's the man.

NEWTON
Peculiar chap, met him once.
Cromwell's Foreign Secretary.
Good job he isn't here, though.
He'd never stop talking. Politics, politics.
Poet as well, was he?

(pause)

DARWIN *(slowly)*
I had a strange dream once—
Listening to Tennyson's poetry reminded me of it.
I dreamt someone gave me a book.
It was in German. I started to read the first page.
I understood every word as it came.
But when I got to the end of the page,
I didn't understand what the *page* was about.
Nothing. I went through the whole book like that.

NEWTON
Like life, I suppose. I'm glad it's over.

DARWIN
It's not much different now.
Just a longer book. Eternal Tennyson.

(pause. Tennyson does not moan from now on)

NEWTON *(thoughtfully)*
I had a strange dream myself once.
At least, I think it was a dream.
I met God. At least, I think it was God.
I was in my laboratory—doing my tax returns,
in fact. This gentle old man came in
and said he wanted my help with a problem.
He'd heard I was a scientist.
He took me off to his house, somewhere.
I don't remember. But there was a magnificent
laboratory there, every instrument you could wish
for. He showed me in, and pointed to a large grey
ball on a workbench. Covered with dust.
Obviously been there for ages.
"I've been trying for a very long time to discover
what that's made of," he said.
"Could you please analyse it for me?"
I remember he said "please."
I said I'd try and he left me there. So I got to work.
It was all quite simple really. In a few hours,
I had a list of all the chemicals, the minerals,
the gases, all neatly tabulated and classified.
When he came back he seemed very pleased.
He went through the list, checking off each
element. But when he'd finished, he turned to me,
rather sadly and said: "But what about the dust?"
"The dust?" I said. "The dust on the globe" he said.
"Oh, I brushed that off before I started work,"
I said. "That's a pity," he said.
And then I woke up. I think.

DARWIN *(quietly)*
Dust to dust.

NEWTON
That's what I thought.

(pause)

NEWTON
Tennyson's gone quiet.
I'm going to try to get some sleep.

DARWIN
(sotto voce:) Perchance to dream.
(aloud:) Good night, Isaac, sleep well.

NEWTON
And you.

(pause)

NEWTON *(quietly)*
Do corpses sleep, Charles?

DARWIN
Plants do. *(slight pause)* And worms.
Thank God.
Good night, Newton.

NEWTON
Good night, Darwin, Good night.

(slight pause)

*A yellow tennis ball bounces languidly across the stage
from stage right to stage left,
bouncing perhaps 3 or 4 times,
and disappears into the wings.*

Spots fade out.

Close of play.

*

www.ingramcontent.com/pod-product-compliance
Lightning Source LLC
Chambersburg PA
CBHW071901020426
42331CB00010B/2613